YOUR FEELINGS...

or

**Biblical Guidelines
For Managing
Your Emotions**

Dr. RICHARD D. DOBBINS

Lovingly dedicated to Priscilla,
a precious gift from God
who has touched my feelings and
won my heart.

April, 1994

Table of Contents

Introduction

This book addresses one of the most important potential benefits of our Christian stewardship: our mental health.

As Christians, the quality of our lives affects the credibility of our testimony. A vibrant, healthy faith in Christ should be expressed in a celebration of life that is obvious to those around us, as Paul recorded in Romans 14:17 (KJV):

> *"For the kingdom of God is not meat and drink, but righteousness, and peace, and joy in the Holy Ghost."*

Professing this kingdom without enjoying it is the pathetic plight of many who have not yet discovered the vital link between spiritual experience and mental health.

The Bible says we are made in the image of God (Genesis 1:27). Scripture reveals God to be One who *feels* as well as *thinks*. So, being made in His image means that we are *feeling* persons as well as *thinking* persons. In fact, you and I experience life through both our feelings and our thoughts. However, we have

i

been taught to pay much more attention to our thoughts than to our feelings. *We have few opportunities to define our feelings, learn how to label them, and discover how to live with them.* Particularly in our early years of life, much of our time is spent in schools primarily dedicated to teaching us how to *think.*

It is encouraging to see so many pastors and church leaders respond to our tremendous need to more clearly understand our feelings and to develop Biblical ways of expressing them. The church is at last awakening to its role in providing us opportunities to learn about our feelings and how to live with them.

The stewardship of our feelings affects every relationship of our lives. This is true whether we are male or female, young or old, married or single. Learning the origins of our feelings, becoming aware of how we experience them, and developing Biblical ways of managing them can only *enrich* our personal lives and *benefit* our interpersonal relationships. In this book you will discover—or perhaps rediscover—the vital relationship between your faith and your mental health.

In Chapter One, we'll look at how a healthy faith in God enables you to develop and maintain healthy ways of dealing with life in general. Then, over the next five chapters, we will deal with specific problem areas that I have seen trouble God's people again and again in the more than thirty-five years I have been counseling Christians. These are emotional concerns that give *all of us* problems from time to time: self-concept, fear and anxiety, anger, guilt, and depression.

Of the five areas mentioned, a poor self-concept is the most common. Often this problem results from improper and/or poorly understood religious training during childhood. We address this issue in Chapter Two, and introduce a model for bringing your confusion and hurts to God in prayer for the guidance and healing you need.

Some of the most remarkable emotional healings I have ever witnessed—or experienced—have come through these times of private, personal prayer when difficult issues of life have been "prayed through."

Next, we approach two closely related subjects: fear and anxiety. These painful emotions also have their roots in early childhood. Fear and anxiety are the first emotions infants experience. And anxiety disorders are one of the most common areas of complaint among adults seen in counseling.

Anger—the subject of Chapter Four—is particularly difficult for many Christians to accept. These people believe that any expression of anger is a contradiction of their faith. Nevertheless, we frequently see people from a broad segment of the church whose major problem is anger management. Of course, anger doesn't have to present the believer with such an overwhelming challenge. It can be a positive, healthy force in the believer's life, but it does have to be properly managed. We'll look at how anger affects one's health and relationships and explore some methods for constructively managing it.

Chapter Five offers a look at the distinct differences between healthy and unhealthy guilt. A healthy conscience and healthy guilt enable people to live together in society; an unhealthy conscience and unhealthy guilt can create all kinds of problems within and among people. We'll talk about both healthy and unhealthy guilt; how to identify and resolve each.

In Chapter Six, we will explore ways believers can manage their bouts with depression. This is the most common of all emotional problems, afflicting an estimated 50 million Americans annually. Many of them are believers. Although the stress of modern living has certainly contributed to the present epidemic proportions of depression, it is not new or unique to our generation. As we will see, depression has been with us since Bible times.

Chapter Seven wraps up our study with a look at how closely the emotional and spiritual dimensions of our lives are related. Each impacts upon and interacts with the other in ways that deeply affect the manner in which we experience *all* dimensions of our lives. This book is written to help us understand the nature of this interaction more clearly.

Our feelings about ourselves, our families, and life in general are formed very *subtly* and very *early* in life—long before we start to school. The spiritual experience each of us has a little farther along into life both *grows out of* and *is affected by* these earlier realities.

Unhealthy religious experience, just like mental illness or other emotional disturbance (whether experienced in childhood or adulthood), distorts the way we see *ourselves* and *others—* including *God.* On the other hand, a *healthy* spiritual experience can be an *effective therapeutic resource* for helping the mentally ill and emotionally disturbed regain their mental health.

When our spiritual experience and religious beliefs are consistent with healthy views of God, self, and others, they help minimize our emotional pain and maximize our pleasures in life. I sincerely hope this book will assist you in achieving this level of spiritual and emotional health—which is your spiritual birthright.

Throughout the book are descriptions of common—but very painful—problems people have brought to EMERGE in counseling. Of course, people's names, circumstances, and other identifying data have been altered and disguised so that client confidentiality is protected. In an effort to help you understand what may be happening in your own life or the life of someone close to you, I have shared these experiences with you.

Many people fear any information or "wisdom" which they do not perceive as being directly from God's Word or a personal revelation of God's truth. During my years of study and preparation in a secular university, I had to come to terms with this same kind of uncertainty. God helped me tool out a way of deciding what I could accept from the behavioral sciences that I'd like to share with you here.

First of all, much that is offered by the behavioral sciences contradicts Scripture. This can never be a part of the believer's counseling practice or personal belief system.

There is, however, also much that—while not clearly supportive of Scripture—is at least not contradictory. And a large body of scientific wisdom is consistent with and clearly supportive of Scripture. From *this* body of information, the behavioral sciences serve to help the believer discover practical ways to apply God's wisdom* and His truth to life situations—ways that are consistent with His Word.

In the final analysis, wisdom—wherever it is found—is of God. Whether it comes to us filtered through the best information of the behavioral sciences or directly as revealed through His Word and during times of private prayer, it is still His wisdom and His truth. We have His Word on that:

> *"For the LORD giveth wisdom: out of his mouth cometh knowledge and understanding"* (Proverbs 2:6, KJV).

It is my hope that this book will help you discover healthier ways of living with your feelings through practical applications of a healthy faith in God. As you begin your study, please pause a moment and ask God to help you make these truths from His Word and His servant a permanent part of your life. Allow this text to minister to you in your own time of need, and then please share it with a friend!

Richard D. Dobbins, Ph.D.

Chapter 1

How Healthy is Your Faith?

Ten Ways to Test Your Faith

In its 1978 report, the President's Commission on Mental Health warned that if the social trends of that time continued, one in seven people living in the United States would require treatment for some kind of emotional disturbance during his or her lifetime.

Why has our national environment become so threatening to our mental health? Let's look at some of the factors.

The current rate of technological change is mind-boggling. Advances in science, technology, and industry have placed at our disposal such rapid means of transportation and communication that we are exposed to as many life experiences in a *year* as previous generations knew in a *lifetime*. We stagger under the impact of information and stimulation overload.

For example, many of us travel twenty miles to work each day. After a round trip of forty miles and working eight hours,

1

we may go out with family or friends for an evening of entertainment. At the beginning of this century, just traveling forty miles would have consumed the entire day. Before we had radio and television, news of events at a distance took weeks to reach us. And even then, our grasp of their reality was limited to the relatively new art of photography and the vivid imagery of printed news accounts of what happened. Today, the marriage of telephone, radio, television, microwave, and computer technologies combined can deliver to our homes each morning and evening all of the misery of the whole world— in stereo sound and living color.

The speed of life, the rapid rate of change, the almost endless variety of options from which we may choose a lifestyle, the anonymous quality of life in our rootless society where half of the population moves every five years . . . these are just some of the factors which combine to plague us with moral confusion and spiritual conflict.

In the midst of all of this, we attempt to give our lives meaning and direction.

Unparalleled social change.

The family is undergoing a radical change. Marriages are falling apart at a record pace. Over 50 percent of first marriages now end in divorce. Estimates indicate that 70 percent of our children will spend some of their developmental years in a single-parent family.

The enormity of this family disintegration trend becomes obvious in documents like the 1991 report from Ohio's Department of Education. When high school seniors in this midwestern state registered for classes in the fall of 1991, 77 percent gave different names for parental figures in their homes than the names they registered when they entered kindergarten. Only 23 percent of Ohio's teens who were graduating in 1992

2

had the same parental figures in the home they had when they started kindergarten!

We live in a very sick society.

Is it any wonder that a veritable flood of emotional disturbance is sweeping across America? Every year well over 50 million people suffer mild to moderate depression. Another 2 million are deeply depressed; 20 million are neurotic; 10 million have serious alcohol problems; 10 million have been arrested for crimes; 6 million children and youth are emotionally disturbed; 1 million students withdraw from school because of emotional problems; 1 million are actively schizophrenic; 200,000 attempt suicide; 200,000 cases of child abuse are reported. Suicide is now the second highest cause of death among our teenagers, second only to accidental deaths—which are often suspected of being suicides disguised as accidents. In 1986, 18 percent of teenage girls and 10 percent of teenage boys in America tried to commit suicide.

Free-standing psychiatric hospitals are rapidly becoming the new social dumping grounds for adolescents whose parents can no longer manage them. In 1971, only 6,500 of our American youth were in psychiatric wards. Today, over 200,000 of them are there. And 80 percent of these young people are from homes broken by divorce.

In their frantic efforts to cope with unparalleled stress, increasing numbers of Americans are turning to some form of substance abuse. Every day, tons of tranquilizers, anti-depressants, anti-psychotic agents, and sleeping pills are being consumed by troubled people in our society. What a commentary on today's America!

Psychotropic (mood-altering) drugs, properly administered and supervised by physicians, do play a major role in the treatment of mental illness. They do have a legitimate role as

3

temporary support for people under stress. Unfortunately, many people are seeking a permanent solution to their emotional problems in prescription medications, over-the-counter drugs, and other abused substances.

Believers are not immune to our society's emotional risks. In fact, in the New Testament, Paul warns readers about the dangers of the crumbling social and emotional climate of the last days. He writes in 2 Timothy 3:1-4 (KJV):

"This know also, that in the last days perilous times shall come. For men shall be lovers of their own selves, covetous, boasters, proud, blasphemers, disobedient to parents, unthankful, unholy, without natural affection, truce breakers, false accusers, incontinent, fierce, despisers of those that are good, traitors, heady, high-minded, lovers of pleasure more than lovers of God."

In the past, ministers and psychologists tended to view their respective fields as antithetical—like oil and water. Religion and psychology, according to many of them, just didn't mix. Some still feel that way. Today, however, there is evidence that an increasing number of reputable people from both camps are looking at their old viewpoint with a careful eye.

They are beginning to see the benefit of helping the minister better understand the emotional issues involved in a person's religious experience, and of helping the psychologist or psychiatrist better understand the spiritual issues involved in a person's emotional life.

Your faith and emotions are intertwined.

Because they affect us eternally, the issues of our faith are much more important to us than the psychological issues of life. Nevertheless, we need all the help both fields can provide in our effort to stay mentally healthy in our sick society.

4

When I began my Christian life as a teenager, mental health was certainly not one of my major concerns. Since both of my parents had been active in church all my life, I believed I had grown up in a normal family.

At that time, I simply didn't understand how good Christian people could have emotional problems. The prevailing belief in our church and in many others was that when a person became a Christian everything about that person was totally, miraculously changed—including their personal history.

The conversion experience was further believed to take care of everything necessary to provide one with the same kind of future a person who grew up in an emotionally healthy home could look forward to—regardless of how destructive his or her early life might have been. And, once a person became a Christian, the daily habits of prayer and Bible reading were believed able to protect them from painful emotional problems.

This theology was taught openly at times and implied at other times. And I believed what I was taught.

Years later, when I looked back on my early life, I realized I had brought into my Christian life many unresolved mental health issues from my family. I also began to recognize major mental health problems in other members of my family who were Christians. I began to realize that the purpose of sanctification was to help Christians deal redemptively with this kind of pain and confusion from their past. But at the time of my conversion, I was totally unaware that I *had* any emotional problems.

Faith in Christ helps you deal with your past.

My personal decision to follow Christ came during a typical evangelistic invitation given by my pastor following his Sunday evening message. I had listened to his stirring sermon on the brevity of life and the certainty of judgment.

5

At the time, I knew I wasn't the world's greatest sinner, but I also knew that many of my activities were contrary to what my church and family had taught me. Additional guilt fell on me for involving my girlfriend in kinds of entertainment both of us had been taught were wrong.

My resistance to the preacher's appeal broke when my girlfriend reached over to return my high school class ring which I had given to her as a token of my love. She told me that until I became a Christian, she could no longer be my girlfriend.

When that kind of leverage was added to the guilt I felt already, it was enough to send me to the altar. That night I prayed the sinner's prayer. Everyone there rejoiced with me, because I had given my life to Christ. I still look back on that as the wisest decision in my life, but now I understand there were many factors in my motivation other than simply responding to the pastor's sermon and yielding to Christ's claims on my life.

That decision not only resolved my major conflict with sin, it also relieved tension between me and my family, reconciled me to my girlfriend, and gave me the spiritual resources I needed to come to terms with pains from my past.

To this day, I am unsure which of those several pressures exerted the most influence on my decision for Christ. This is how tightly the spiritual, emotional, and social issues of life are intertwined. And more and more, professionals from the fields of religion and the behavioral sciences are beginning to understand this.

Unhealthy faith—unhealthy feelings.

An unhealthy religious experience can be detrimental to your mental health. You will be able to see this in Myrtle's life as I share her story with you. Of course, that's not her real name. Her husband (we'll call him George) became concerned about

Myrtle when she came home from a prayer meeting and told him that Jesus was calling her into a special life of prayer.

After that, George began to notice that Myrtle was starting to neglect their home. She had been an immaculate housekeeper. Now, when he came home from work in the evening, the dishes from breakfast were still on the table. The beds weren't made. Their two boys, ages seven and nine, obviously had been allowed to run through the house all day as they pleased. None of these things seemed to bother Myrtle.

When George brought these things to her attention, she cried and complained that he just didn't understand her. She lamented over his lack of spiritual commitment. Not long after that, she began sleeping in another bedroom so she wouldn't awaken him when she got up to pray. Of course, that also made it easier for her to avoid what she called George's "carnal advances."

George knew something was happening to his wife. But he didn't know what it was or what to do about it. Finally, he talked to the minister in charge of the prayer meeting Myrtle had been attending. The minister agreed that her actions were strange; however, he attributed her behavior to the fact that spiritual experience was a relatively new thing for Myrtle. He encouraged George to be patient and assured him that his wife's rather fanatical emphasis on prayer would soon level off.

The minister promised to have a talk with Myrtle. He did talk to her right away, but it didn't seem to help. Instead, she took offense at what the minister said and chided him for not being more spiritual. She began to get up even earlier in the morning for her prayer time.

George became furious with her when he discovered her waking their sons at five o'clock in the morning to pray with her. When he asked her to explain, she calmly told him Jesus had appeared to her in a vision and told her to include the boys in her

7

early morning prayer because He was calling them to be ministers. At this point, George made a wise but difficult decision. He sought professional help for Myrtle. At first, she wanted nothing to do with psychiatric help. She decided to come only when her husband convinced her that the people at our center would understand her faith. She agreed to see me.

In the first session I had with Myrtle, she was very anxious to determine whether or not Jesus was real to me. Being assured that He was, she told me about her own encounter with Christ in great detail. Of course, for her it was very real. But it was also a very emotionally disintegrative and disabling experience for her.

Healthy faith integrates you.

A healthy religious experience is never disintegrative. It is never disabling. In fact, just the opposite is true. It is always integrative. It always enables us to function better. In Myrtle's case, a healthy religious experience would have helped her function more effectively as a wife, mother, and homemaker. To a trained observer, the disintegrative nature of her spiritual experience marked it as being very unhealthy.

Taking great pains to reinforce healthy parts of her faith, I assured Myrtle that *although her symptoms were religious, her problem was emotional.* I asked if she had recently experienced some emotional shock or major personal loss. She confided in me that her father had died recently and her best friend had been killed in a tragic automobile accident about six months prior to the time she came to see me.

Myrtle was overwhelmed by these losses. It is impossible for any healthy person to suffer the deaths of two important people in their world and not be emotionally affected in some way.

8

I suggested to George that the boys be cared for by another member of the family for a few weeks. Myrtle was hospitalized. During her five-week hospital stay, she was given a combination of medicine, Biblical counseling, and rest. Under these conditions and the supervision of our staff psychiatrist, Myrtle made good progress.

After she was released from the hospital, she and George resumed their life together as they had known it before. Gradually, Myrtle regained her ability to care for their two healthy boys and their home.

I continued to see her for counseling until she had worked through her grief and learned some new, healthy ways of applying her faith to her daily life experiences. She learned how to tell the difference between a healthy and an unhealthy religious experience so she didn't need to become afraid of her faith—or fear that the nightmare of her emotional disturbance would return.

Not all forms of Christianity are emotionally healthy.

This should come as no surprise to students of the faith. Sick forms of the Christian religion have been around for two thousand years. John writes about the immature believer who is overwhelmed with fear and insecurity (1 John 4:18). Paul writes about a form of Christianity that manipulates and preys on innocent people, and is practiced by *"the sleight of men, and cunning craftiness, whereby they lie in wait to deceive"* (Ephesians 4:14, KJV).

In both of these references, the apostles are dealing with people whose faith has secured them a place in heaven—but they continue to have a miserable time getting there. When your faith is both Biblically sound and emotionally healthy, you will not only make it to heaven; you will also enjoy your trip. You can't beat that combination. Why settle for less?

9

Now that we've talked about the problem of unhealthy faith, you may be wondering how to determine whether some of the religious experiences people have are mentally healthy or unhealthy. Is there a way to tell?

If you read the introduction to this book, you noticed I said God is the source of all wisdom. As the author of our faith, He has provided in His Word guidelines for keeping our faith healthy. It is to our benefit to become sufficiently familiar with Scripture to know when it is being interpreted in ways contrary to our mental health.

In order to be a good steward of a healthy faith, we need Biblical ways of testing religious ideas before we open ourselves to them. Often, in our mass-media world, we are confronted with many sick forms of religion that are made to appear quite appealing. But Paul, in 1 Corinthians 14:29 (KJV), reminds us how important it is to carefully judge the words of anyone who would try to influence us spiritually. He says, quite bluntly, *"Let the prophets speak two or three, and let the others judge."*

What does he mean by that? As we listen to people who speak to us from the Scripture, we should develop ways of determining how Biblically sound and healthy their teachings are.

Ten ways to test your faith . . .

With Paul's words in mind, let's take a look at some practical and Biblical guidelines for helping people discern the difference between a healthy faith and one that is unhealthy. I have defined these guidelines from my years of clinical experience with God's people who were wrestling with a number of unhealthy religious views. I can assure you this kind of mental insurance is extremely important for Christians.

Many of the emotionally troubled people who come to me for help are suffering from symptoms brought on by unhealthy religious experiences or beliefs. Applying these guidelines to your faith can spare you the pain and confusion of an unhealthy faith and help you to reap all the benefits of a healthy faith.

1. Healthy faith is affirmed in fellowship.

Beware of isolated religious groups that insist on rigid conformity to strange beliefs and practices which have little if any Biblical support. Remember, Paul admonished Timothy to display reputable scholarship in his approach to Biblical interpretations, so that he might *"rightly divide"* (or present) *"the word of truth"* (2 Timothy 2:15, KJV). Also, Peter warns the believer that, *". . . no prophecy of the scripture is of any private interpretation"* (2 Peter 1:20, KJV).

Christianity provides a wide variety of church groups which can be identified by their honest differences. These are distinguished from each other by different scholarly interpretations of portions of the Bible. If our faith is healthy, we should be able to identify theologically with at least one of these groups. When a person's beliefs are so unique and different that they are unable to find any group of fellow believers with whom they are comfortable, their beliefs are suspect. Remember, Jesus wants His followers to be one with Him and with one another.

That is the subject of His priestly prayer as recorded in John 17:21 (KJV):

"That they all may be one; as thou, Father, art in me, and I in thee, that they also may be one in us: that the world may believe that thou hast sent me."

2. Healthy faith sees God as love.

None of us relates to God as He is. We relate to Him as we have Him pictured in our minds. Many believers still picture God as angry with them. They seek to avoid His wrath. They feel His

11

approval is beyond their reach. They are unaware of His constant care for them. We'll take a better look at how this affects a believer's other relationships in Chapter 4, where we discuss: "Anger: Master or Servant?"

Often, when believers view God as angry and wrathful, they are placing too strong an emphasis on an Old Testament view of God. They see Him only as an angry judge. And it is true that God presided over the flood, the destruction of wickedness in Sodom and Gomorrah, and the expulsion of the Canaanites. But He is the same God Who presided over the birth, death, and resurrection of His Son, our Lord and Saviour Jesus Christ, as His love gift to you and me.

Each of us has to choose the mental picture of God on which we will focus. Philip was having trouble making the selection, so he said to Jesus, *"Lord, show us the Father, and it sufficeth us."* And Jesus answered him by saying, *"Have I been so long time with you, and yet hast thou not known me, Philip? He that hath seen me hath seen the Father"* (John 14:8,9, KJV). When healthy believers wonder what God is like, they think of Jesus.

3.   Healthy faith fosters self-worth.

No other religion in the world places as much value on an individual as does the Christian faith. Jesus declares that if it were possible to gain the whole world in exchange for your own soul, what you lost would be worth more than what you gained (Mark 8:36,37). What a statement of an individual's worth! And it is the payment of Christ's blood as the price of our redemption that attributes such worth to every human being (1 Peter 1:18).

Every human being is a sinner. Scripture insists that we be honest about our sins . . . with God and with ourselves. 1 John 1:8 (KJV) declares, *"If we say that we have no sin, we deceive ourselves, and the truth is not in us."*

12

God assures us of His love (Romans 5:7,8, KJV) in spite of our sins:

"For scarcely for a righteous man will one die: yet peradventure for a good man some would even dare to die. But God commendeth his love toward us, in that, while we were yet sinners, Christ died for us."

The fact that the sins of mankind are responsible for the death of God's only begotten Son makes the thought of trivializing even the smallest of sins blasphemy. Yet, realizing that God's sinless Son died for the "ungodly" magnifies His love and grace toward all mankind.

Confession of sin provides the joy of forgiveness.

Confession of sin should lead us to repentance and forgiveness. Nevertheless, some people, even after they have been forgiven, seem to have more of a need to focus on their sorrow for sin than on their joy of forgiveness. When I focus on my sinfulness, I feel horrible about myself. And yet, I want to be honest about my sins. I can't forget John's admonition: *"If we say that we have no sin, we deceive ourselves, and the truth is not in us."* But he also adds, remember, *"If we confess our sins, he is faithful and just to forgive us our sins, and to cleanse us from all unrighteousness"* (1 John 1:8,9, KJV).

Once I have honestly confessed my sins to Jesus, I no longer want to think about them. Instead, I want to focus on the joy of my forgiveness and how much God loves me. And . . . how much is that?

God loves His children "much more" than Calvary.

If you want to know how much God loves you as His child, the next time you see a cross, remind yourself that the cross does not fully express the magnitude of God's love for His *children.* The cross only demonstrates for us how much God

13

loves the unsaved—His *enemies*. Paul put it this way in Romans 5:10 (KJV):

> *"For if, when we were enemies, we were reconciled to God by the death of his Son; much more, being reconciled, we shall be saved by his life."*

So, remember, the cross only helps us grasp God's love for us when we were His enemies. To even begin to understand just how much He loves us now that we are His children, envision in capital letters the words "MUCH MORE" written above the cross. Then you have some idea just how much God loves each of His children—including you. That discovery can make a world of difference in the way you view yourself. It also affects the way you feel about God, as we'll see in the next chapter.

So, remember, Calvary does not tell us how much God loves His children. It reveals God's love for His enemies. He loves His child ... MUCH MORE!

4.   Healthy faith meets reality.

At any given moment, reality for each of us is a personal combination of past influences, present stresses, and their interactions with each other. These influences and stresses are fourfold in nature: physical, psychological, social, and spiritual.

Such areas of influence and stress tend to impact on each other. For example, in our culture we expect men to be taller than women. Therefore, a man who is genetically determined to be short or a woman who is going to be tall will experience emotional and social stress as a result of this physical factor in their life.

Being born into poverty or wealth is a social fact of life over which we have no control. However, such an event can have a profound effect on the physical, psychological, and spiritual dimensions of one's life. The sudden loss of wealth, position, or a loved one can trigger functional depression (the kind resulting

14

from situational stress) which drastically affects the physical, social, and even spiritual dimension of life.

It should be obvious that most of us bring from our past some events and experiences which could adversely affect our mental health. In addition, all of us must risk stresses from our present which could devastate us. There simply is no life without storms.

In the closing illustration of His Sermon on the Mount, Jesus guarantees the survival of His followers who respond to life's storms as He has taught them—but predicts disaster for those who don't:

"Therefore, whosoever heareth these sayings of mine, and doeth them, I will liken him unto a wise man, which built his house upon a rock: And the rain descended, and the floods came, and the winds blew, and beat upon that house; and it fell not: for it was founded upon a rock. And every one that heareth these sayings of mine, and doeth them not, shall be likened unto a foolish man, which built his house upon the sand: And the rain descended, and the floods came, and the winds blew, and beat upon that house; and it fell: and great was the fall of it."

(Matthew 7:24-27, KJV)

Each of us creates a story about life's storms!

This helps explain why some people are so severely damaged by life, while others survive and even thrive in the face of adversity. At times, life deals potentially crippling blows to each of us. But what happens to us is not nearly as critical to our emotional and spiritual health as is the way we choose to react to what happens.

More important to your mental health than influences from your past or stresses from your present is the way you have learned to *talk to yourself* about these things. *None of us live*

15

simply with what we experience in life. We live with the way we choose to feel and think about what we experience. The facts of our experiences are not as critical to our mental health as the meanings we assign those facts.

We teach ourselves stories about the facts of our lives. And after we have learned these stories well, we tell them to ourselves over and over again. The images and feelings these stories create in our minds are what we live with.

Solomon wisely observed this when he wrote, *"For as he thinketh in his heart, so is he"* (Proverbs 23:7, KJV). Each of us uniquely perceives his circumstances and responds to them. This accounts for the many different ways people in any given family are affected by the same set of family circumstances even though they share the same home.

In my work as a therapist, I make it very clear to hurting people that no one can ever change what has happened to them. However, if they are willing to work at it, I can help them find a way of *feeling* and *thinking* about what has happened to them that won't hurt so much.

Part of this healing is accomplished by a process of creative prayer. The four steps to "praying through" such a situation are discussed in Chapter 2 and again in Chapter 7. A healthy faith allows you to engage in creative prayer and discover new ways of looking at what has happened to you. It helps you to learn a less destructive version of the painful chapters of your life.

Do you remember the story of Joseph? His brothers envied him and would have killed him had it not been for the chance to sell him into slavery. How do you like that for brotherly love? Once in Egypt, his master's wife had Joseph falsely charged and thrown in prison for not giving in to her seductive ways. Can you imagine how it must have felt to go to jail for doing what was right? Once in jail, Joseph was forgotten by his friend—the butler who had promised to remember Joseph when he was restored to Pharaoh's favor. Still, in the face of all this, Joseph refused to become bitter or seek revenge.

In Genesis 50:15-21 (KJV), Moses preserves this beautiful example of Joseph's mentally healthy faith for us:

"And when Joseph's brethren saw that their father was dead, they said, Joseph will peradventure hate us, and will certainly requite us all the evil which we did unto him. And they sent a messenger unto Joseph, saying, Thy father did command before he died, saying, So shall ye say unto Joseph, Forgive, I pray thee now, the trespass of thy brethren, and their sin; for they did unto thee evil: and now, we pray thee, forgive the trespass of the servants of the God of thy father. And Joseph wept when they spake unto him. And his brethren also went and fell down before his face; and they said, Behold, we be thy servants. And Joseph said unto them, Fear not: for am I in the place of God? But as for you, ye thought evil against me; but God meant it unto good, to bring to pass, as it is this day, to save much people alive. Now therefore fear ye not; I will nourish you, and your little ones. And he comforted them, and spake kindly unto them."

Joseph had little or no control over what happened to him during those horror-filled years as a slave and prisoner in Egypt. However, he determined to stay in control of how he permitted himself to feel and think about the injustices of those years. He knew that bitterness never hurts those who cause it as much as it does those who harbor it.

5. Healthy faith cushions "future shock."

Alvin Toffler, in his book, **Future Shock**, explains the mounting levels of stress created by the many interlocking drives and forces of Western man's history. People once were separated

17

by natural boundaries, so that events in one part of the world had little or no effect on those who lived in other parts. Little by little, man's genius for inventing methods of transportation and communication has overcome those boundaries. Today, it is impossible to be sheltered from events in other parts of the world by rivers, mountains, deserts, or oceans. What happens on one part of the planet immediately impacts on the people of every other civilized part of the planet. We really do live in a "global village."

The pace of change in our society has also been picking up speed dramatically since the turn of the century. Ask any senior citizen to describe the changes which have taken place in his or her lifetime. It will amaze you.

They have seen our means of travel go from a horse-and-buggy or train to include automobiles, airplanes, and space rockets. They have had to adapt to rapidly changing methods of communication which now include fax machines, computers, and television, with live satellite transmissions of any newsworthy event now being brought right into the home. When our senior citizens were children, it often took *weeks* for news of world tragedy to reach them. Even then, the descriptions were limited to newspaper accounts and a few black-and-white pictures. Now news can be transmitted from any spot on earth right into their homes *in living color right at the moment it is happening.*

Our elders have watched as the rural way of life so familiar to them has been swallowed up by land-hungry cities and eight-lane super-highways. Sprawling farmhouses and rolling pastures have been replaced by high-rise apartments and condominiums with just occasional scattered spots of green city parks.

The pace of the future will continue to accelerate.

Don't look for *the speed of change* to slacken. The one thing about the future which is most predictable is that the pace of change will continue to accelerate. The wedding of telephone and computer technology is just beginning to make its impact on communications. And we have yet to see what supersonic air travel and the space shuttle will do for public transportation.

Failure to emotionally keep pace with and adapt to these ever-increasing changes results in what Toffler called "future shock." In the face of this rapid acceleration, many believers are struggling with crippling levels of tension, worry, and anxiety. Some are trying desperately to deny the daily realities of their world, standing firm on the conviction that they must not change.

Faith is expressed in flexibility.

Healthy faith helps believers adapt to change. Nevertheless, some forms of religious orthodoxy are characterized by a style of thinking which is rigid and inflexible. People who hold to this kind of belief are very uncomfortable in the face of change. In fact, they take pride in their intransigence.

Listening to them, you would think that the less a person changes, the more like God he is. In defense of their refusal to change, these believers often quote Malachi 3:6 (KJV), *"For I am the LORD, I change not,"* and Hebrews 13:8 (KJV), *"Jesus Christ the same yesterday, and today, and forever."*

I have talked to many Christians victimized by this kind of teaching. I have tried to help them become more flexible in their thinking by suggesting that since none of us is God or Jesus, we cannot afford the luxury of remaining the same. We must be open to change.

Of course, there is a healthy fear of any change which would compromise our relationship to Jesus Christ. Sometimes the graduate students in our counseling courses experience this kind of fear. They are afraid of the changes that occur as a result of the intellectual challenge and self-examination graduate studies

19

demand. *They have to be reassured that a healthy faith can accommodate a growing person.*

I understand their dilemma, because I also grew up in a religious environment that taught me to be suspicious of change. I experienced that same kind of anxiety when I was stretching and growing out of some of the unhealthy ideas of my early faith. God helped me define, for my own reassurance at that time in my life, a statement about faith, growth, and change. I share that with our students to reassure them, and I'd like to share it here with you:

To live is to grow. To grow is to change. If one cannot discern the difference between the change that results from growth and the change that results from the loss of one's faith, his fear of losing his faith makes him resist all change. Then his faith becomes an inhibitor of, rather than a facilitator of, his growth.

Do you know of any living thing that isn't growing? Do you know of any growing thing that isn't changing? It is never God's will for our faith to get in the way of our growth. Healthy growth *decreases* the distance between us and God. The more we learn about life, the more in awe of God we are. Our love for God grows greater. We are seized by an intense desire to know Him.

Inflexibility limits one's usefulness to God.

Unless Saul of Tarsus had been willing to risk growing out of the rigid, inflexible mindset of the Pharisees, he never could have become Paul—the apostle to the Gentiles. Before his conversion, he was so legalistic he said he was "blameless" as far as the law of the Pharisees was concerned (Philippians 3:6). You can't get much more religiously rigid than that!

However, once Christ transformed his mind, Paul became so comfortable with the change that he was able and willing to be made *"all things to all men, that [he] might by all means save some"* (1 Corinthians 9:22, KJV). More will be said about that transforming miracle in Chapter 5 when we discuss guilt.

Some things never change.

When your faith is healthy, you understand that in the midst of our rapidly changing world *some things do not change.* For example, *God's person* remains the same (Malachi 3:6). *His Word* never changes (Psalm 119:89,160). *"Jesus Christ [is] the same: yesterday, and today, and forever"* (Hebrews 13:8, KJV). These three immutable truths help to guide the child of God through the tempest of today's relative morality.

Like a good navigator, with your sights on these three fixed points of reference, you can steer your course through the murky waters of our sea of moral uncertainty and creatively manage any changes you must face. You can grow through change when your faith is healthy.

6. Healthy faith manages stress and anxiety.

The stress and anxiety of our fast-paced world don't have to be destructive. Dr. Hans Selye, world-renowned specialist on stress, has coined the word "eustress" to describe how the energy created by stress can be converted into productive, creative activities.

Not only is it *unrealistic* for us to expect to live totally free of stress and anxiety—it is probably *impossible.* In fact, certain amounts of both stress and anxiety are essential elements in times of excitement, motivation, and growth in life. How boring life would be without these moments! A little test anxiety motivates the student to study more, which usually results in a better grade. Entertainers and athletes expect to feel some tension and anxiety just before they go into action. It helps them perform better.

However, large doses of tension and anxiety can cripple a person. Under certain circumstances, the phobic person is

21

literally paralyzed by his anxiety. And I have seen people so overwhelmed by fear that they were unable to leave the security of their home without a family member or friend accompanying them. The fear of doing a less-than-perfect job keeps many obsessive-compulsive people from finishing any of the jobs they start. A person suffering from an obsessive fear of dirt or germs may wash his or her hands from fifty to one hundred times a day in an effort to be germ free.

Many people, including Christians, suffer from these or other forms of illness due largely to anxiety. But it doesn't have to be this way. As you learn to order your life according to the teachings of Jesus, the tensions and anxieties of life become more manageable. After all, He taught us not to worry about material things, but to put the kingdom of God first in our lives and trust Him to see that our material needs are met.

> *"So do not worry, saying, 'What shall we eat?' or 'What shall we drink?' or 'What shall we wear?' For the pagans run after all these things, and your heavenly Father knows that you need them. But seek first his kingdom and his righteousness, and all these things will be given to you as well"* (Matthew 6:31–33, NIV).

Most of our worries are related to our physical existence. Most never materialize. That alone should discourage people from worrying. For many, however, it *reinforces* worrying. They believe their worry prevents scary things from happening to them!

If you want to test this, try a little experiment with a group of your friends. Give them all a sheet of paper with the following instructions: "On this sheet of paper, list all the things you have worried about during the past year." After they have finished this task, tell them, "Turn the paper over and list on the back all of these things you worried about which *actually happened.*"

Very few of the things which they worried about really came to pass. But do you think that will cure the real worriers? Of course not. They would be wondering how many more of these things would have happened had they not worried about them! Instead of concluding that worrying was a waste of time and energy, they would be convinced all the more that worrying really helped to protect them from these things.

Worry and fear are notorious thieves of time and energy. In a later chapter, I will be suggesting some practical ways for keeping them from stealing your kingdom potential.

When our faith is healthy, we trust more and worry less. God wants us to be good stewards of our possessions, but none of them are worthy of our anxiety. All of them perish with use. That is why the healthy believer learns to be more concerned about spiritual matters and less concerned with material things:

> *"Wherefore if ye be dead with Christ from the rudiments of the world, why, as though living in the world, are ye subject to ordinances (touch not; taste not; handle not; Which all are to perish with the using;) after the commandments and doctrines of men? . . . If ye then be risen with Christ, seek those things which are above, where Christ sitteth on the right hand of God. Set your affection on things above, not on things on the earth."*
> (Colossians 2:20-22; 3:1,2, KJV)

7. Healthy faith finds joy in giving.

Giving grudgingly doesn't bless anyone. However, unselfish giving is a joy. This spiritual principle has to be experienced before one can believe it. "Try it—you'll like it." This is what God's Word is really saying in Malachi 3:10 (KJV), where we read:

> *"Prove me now herewith, saith the LORD of hosts, if I will not open you the windows of heaven, and pour you out a blessing."*

Giving is contrary to our selfish human nature. We tend to think the greater joy is in receiving. And yet, when parents compare the Christmas memories of their childhood and the joy of having received from their parents with the joys of giving to their own children, there's no question which memories are more joyful. Seeing the happiness that one's giving brings to those who receive is the greater joy by far.

We soon discover that *the return on our giving* is related to *the generosity of our giving.* The farmer's world is full of examples of this spiritual principle. If we sow sparingly to the soil, the soil returns to us very little harvest. However, if we sow liberally to the soil, we reap a liberal harvest.

In giving, we become a part of the people to whom we give. We are represented in whatever their life and ministry become. It is in giving that each of us shares in the harvest of another's life. Once this discovery is made, we no longer give grudgingly or out of necessity. We give from the heart, knowing that *"God loveth a cheerful giver"* (2 Corinthians 9:7, KJV).

8.   Healthy faith manages anger constructively.

No one lives without anger. You may be so threatened by anger that you learn ways of hiding it from yourself. You may even deny it. Nevertheless, you still experience it.

Over a long period of time, hidden anger can be very damaging. If you impulsively act out your anger, you take unnecessary risks which often complicate your life. If you displace your anger (express it toward someone you fear less than the person who provoked your anger in the first place), you are likely to damage important relationships in your life.

You are wiser to think of anger as unexpressed energy. This allows you to understand anger management as energy management. Finding constructive ways to put that energy to work makes anger your friend instead of your enemy.

24

The energy generated by anger can cut grass, scrub floors, drive golf balls, wash walls, and do many other things. Why not put it to work for you? Anger makes a great servant . . . but a poor master. In Chapter 4, you will find a formula for managing anger that has helped many people put anger to work for them.

9. Healthy faith balances work and play.

Both work and play are important mental health issues. The key is balance. Somewhere between "workaholic" and "playboy" there is a blend that is right for you.

Many people are surprised to find out that work is not a part of the curse. When God made man, He gave him a job. Work is essential to health—both physically demanding work and intellectual work. When God created Adam, He gave him the physical task of dressing and caring for the Garden of Eden (Genesis 2:15). He also brought all the animals to Adam and gave him the intellectual task of naming them (Genesis 2:19). We need to work with our bodies and our minds.

We spend more time working than we spend in any other waking activity. This is why it is so important for young people to give careful thought to the kind of work they would find challenging and prepare themselves for it. They should have definite ideas about their future in the work world by the time they finish junior high school. By forming goals like these, they can spare themselves the personal pain and life complications of involvement in drugs and unwanted pregnancies—the all-too-common byproducts of aimless teen years. Young people who do not engage in this kind of career planning allow a major part of their lives to be left to the sheer luck of an unstable job market.

As important as work is, we must remember that God also made man to play. One day in seven He designated for worship, recreation, and rest. We should never be too saintly to enjoy playing.

When I was a child, the fourth commandment was interpreted to mean, "You can't have any fun on Sunday." No play of any kind was permitted. I dreaded Sundays. Please don't misunderstand; I believe worship is the most important activity of the Lord's Day and should have priority over other activities. However, I also believe Sunday is a day for family and recreation. When this balance is kept, children learn to love worship and adults don't forget how to play.

Remember the importance of play to a healthy life and keep your sense of humor. This will go a long way toward sparing you the misery of functional depression—the kind of depression that comes when a person is overwhelmed by the circumstances of life. Of course, some depression is biochemical in nature and not directly related to your circumstances. This kind of depression should be treated biochemically. In Chapter 6, you'll learn some ways to tell the difference between these two kinds of depression. You will read about my first wife's battle with post-partum depression and how God helped her overcome it.

10. Healthy faith loves and forgives others.

Paul reminded young Timothy, *"For God hath not given us the spirit of fear; but of power, and of love, and of a sound mind"* (2 Timothy 1:7, KJV). Notice that love is the second gift mentioned. Power is the first.

The Greek word for power in this verse is "dunamis," which refers to miraculous power or, in some instances, a miracle. In any case, Paul makes it clear to Timothy that God has provided a divine enablement for the believer to help him be a loving and forgiving person.

No one can express true love from a position of weakness—not even Jesus. He came to love His enemies and to lay down His life for them. He was able to manifest this kind of love because He knew that once His enemies had taken His life from Him, His heavenly Father would give Him the power to take it up again. Remember, Jesus said:

"No man taketh [my life] from me, but I lay it down of myself. I have power to lay it down, and I have power to take it again" (John 10:18, KJV).

Often, I see believers trying to live the Christian life without any consciousness of God's divine enablement, simply because it is their Christian duty. How frustrating this must be! One of the evidences of being God's child is the expression of a God-given ability to love:

"We know that we have passed from death unto life, because we love the brethren. He that loveth not his brother abideth in death" (1 John 3:14, KJV).

As you are able to love and forgive, recognize this as God's gift to you. Celebrate it! Express it! And as you do, your ability to love and forgive will expand to include not only your family and friends but also your enemies. Being able to love and forgive your enemies leaves your tomorrows free from the anger, fear, and bitterness of your yesterdays.

There's no healthier way to live!

There is no healthier way to live than the way of life Jesus taught. In fact, if there had been a way to get more out of life, the Bible would have given it to us. It is God's will that His children live life to its fullest. He has given us His Spirit and His Word so that we might know and enjoy creative living—at its best. Several years ago, I discovered some secrets in this regard. In Chapter 7 of this book, I'll be sharing them with you.

Remember, even in our crazy, mixed-up world, believers can enjoy the best of mental health. Your faith is an important part of your mental health. Keep your faith healthy! It will enable you to avoid unnecessary mental health risks, support you in the

27

unavoidable storms of life, and help you celebrate more joyfully when life goes well.

In the following chapter, I want to help you take a close look at your self-image. Your self-image is an important part of your mental health, and your faith is a key ingredient in developing and maintaining a healthy self-image. I will also help you understand more clearly, in that chapter, the relationship between your faith and your self-image.

Chapter 2
You Can Change Your Self-Concept
"Changing the Lens Through Which You Look at Life"

Jerry and Sue had been seeing me for several weeks. Their marriage was in trouble. Sue resented having to assume so much responsibility for family leadership. Whether it was planning their social life, disciplining their three children, or managing the family budget, Sue was the one who was stuck with it. Her way of reacting was to withdraw—emotionally and physically—from Jerry. Their love life had dwindled to almost nothing. It never had been good; in all their married life, Sue had never been orgasmic.

As you might imagine, Sue was the talkative one in our sessions. However, when Jerry did volunteer a comment, I was impressed with his insight and judgment. I remember saying to him, "Jerry, when you do manage to enter into discussion with Sue, your remarks are so helpful. Why don't you talk more?"

Tears filled Jerry's eyes as he replied, "I guess it's because when I was growing up as a kid nobody at home seemed to care

29

what I thought. Us kids were to be 'seen and not heard.' I've grown up believing it was best to keep my opinions to myself."

From that little insight into Jerry's potential, I realized he needed help correcting some seriously mistaken ideas about himself. As we worked together, Jerry discovered that he wasn't dumb. In fact, he was very bright. He learned how important his opinions were to the success of his marriage and worked hard to develop appropriate ways to express them.

Consequently, his behavior in the family changed dramatically. He became more responsive to Sue and more attentive to their children. Sue no longer had to bear the burden of Jerry's passivity. She had always loved him. Now, her respect for him began to grow as well.

Jerry's different view of himself and Sue's new respect for him brought the spark back into their love life. With the help of a more assertive partner, Sue became orgasmic. This new dimension of pleasure intensified the love bond between them.

I wonder how many others (like Jerry), with just a little help in changing the way they see themselves, could get much more out of life and contribute much more to their marriages and families. Only God knows what a difference such increased joy in life would mean to the credibility of their Christian testimony.

Many Christians lack healthy feelings about themselves.

There is no Biblical guarantee that you will automatically receive healthy feelings about yourself when you accept Jesus as your Savior. Some people do; but many do not. In fact, some Christians mistakenly label good feelings about themselves as pride and conceit—traits God despises (Proverbs 21:4).

These people resist any feelings of healthy self-worth and zealously defend their feelings of worthlessness under the guise of being spiritual and Biblical. Often, such believers reek with the odor of spiritual pride but are unaware of it.

30

The price of our redemption establishes our worth.

Both Paul and Peter announce the unthinkable price God paid in order to redeem us from Satan and make us His children:

"Do you not know that your body is a temple of the Holy Spirit, who is in you, whom you received from God? You are not your own; you were bought at a price. Therefore honor God with your body" (1 Cor. 6:19,20, NIV).

"For you know that it was not with perishable things such as silver or gold that you were redeemed from the empty way of life handed down to you from your forefathers, but with the precious blood of Christ, a lamb without blemish or defect" (1 Peter 1:18,19, NIV).

People who truly discover the worth God ascribes to them in Jesus are neither proud nor conceited. In fact, in the process of making this discovery they are humbled to find that such a price was paid for their redemption. This price is what establishes the worth of all God's children. Calvary gives to every human being a value that cannot be expressed in material terms.

Such a discovery comes only through a sincere application of Biblical truth to one's damaged self-image. With this discovery comes a desire to share this same good news with others who still feel their lives are worthless and meaningless.

God's Word gives us many proven prescriptions for achieving and maintaining a healthy self-image. However, prescriptions are powerless to heal unless the medicine is taken according to directions. The truth of Scripture has to be applied if the benefits are to be enjoyed.

When Jerry put God's Word into action in his life, he saw himself, his marriage, and his relationship to his family in a new light. What happened to Jerry can happen to anyone who discovers a new sense of worth in Jesus. *It can happen to you!*

You can learn to have healthy feelings about yourself.

31

Rather than the coincidental result of evolution, the Bible tells us we are made in God's image:

"So God created man in his own image, in the image of God he created him; male and female created he them."

(Genesis 1:27, KJV)

God not only *thinks*—He *feels*. The Scriptures refer frequently to God's thoughts and His feelings. This means that we are "feeling" beings as well as "thinking" beings, because we are made in His image and this is the kind of being God is.

As His offspring, you and I experience life through our thoughts and our feelings. However, we have been taught much more about *how to think* than we have about *how to feel.* All through school there were far fewer opportunities to learn how to live with our feelings than opportunities to learn how to think about life. When *were* we given a chance to learn about our feelings and how to live with them, or how to modify them?

Feelings do make a difference.

More and more, pastors and church leaders are seeing the tremendous need for us to get in touch with our feelings and to learn Biblical ways of managing them. After all, your stewardship of your feelings affects every relationship in your life. Misunderstandings between mates, friction between parents and children, resentments among brothers and sisters, hard feelings among people at church, conflict on the job—all these painful experiences in life are aggravated by and often rooted in our inability to deal well with our feelings.

When I was pastoring, once in a while I would take time in a Sunday evening service to help people focus on their feelings. Usually I would begin this part of the service by saying something like this: "For the next few minutes, I would like for some of you to stand and tell us how you feel God feels about you."

32

Almost inevitably, the first person to speak would begin by saying, "I think God thinks—." Then, I would have to stop them and patiently remind them what their instructions were. They were to tell us how they felt God feels about them; not what they thought God thinks about them.

In spite of hearing what I had said to the previous person, the next person would usually start out the same way. And I would have to stop them, too, and remind them that we were to focus on God's *feelings toward us*, not His *thoughts about us!*

God's feelings for us are on record.

The Scriptures are unmistakably clear on God's love for us:

"You see, at just the right time, when we were still powerless, Christ died for the ungodly. Very rarely will anyone die for a righteous man, though for a good man someone might possibly dare to die. But God demonstrates his own love for us in this: While we were still sinners, Christ died for us. Since we have now been justified by his blood, how much more shall we be saved from God's wrath through him! For if, when we were God's enemies, we were reconciled to him through the death of his Son, how much more, having been reconciled, shall we be saved through his life" (Romans 5:6-10, NIV).

When we begin to understand how deeply God loves us in Jesus, then we want to love Him in return. At that point, love—not fear—becomes the governing emotion in our relationship with God. And love becomes the dominating emotion of our lives. More will be said about this in Chapter Three.

Problems between people generally come from problems within people.

*Inter*personal problems usually begin as *intra*personal problems. That is, problems *between* people usually can be more clearly understood when viewed as problems *within* people.

33

It has been that way ever since Adam. Do you remember how he explained his disobedience to God? *Adam blamed it all on Eve.* When God approached Eve on the subject, she was no more inclined to accept responsibility for her behavior than was Adam. *She blamed it all on the serpent.*

However, where did their problems really begin? *Adam's problems began within Adam,* not with Eve. *Eve's problems began within Eve,* not with the serpent. Their problems were identical. Adam and Eve both chose to disobey God, but neither wanted to assume responsibility for their own disobedience.

Like Adam and Eve, most of us choose to ignore our own responsibility for our problems. That would be too painful for us to face. We would rather make other people responsible for what troubles us. We have an ingenious ability for doing this.

If it's inconvenient to blame our problems on other human beings, we often blame them on the devil. According to legend, Martin Luther had a vision in which he saw the devil sitting by the side of the road crying. In the vision, Luther approached the devil and asked him why he was crying. Satan replied, "Because I get blamed for so many things I'm not responsible for!"

Problems between people usually begin as problems within people. If we were more skilled in identifying and managing problems *within ourselves,* we would have fewer problems *among ourselves.* It is amazing how much brighter the world becomes when we clean our own glasses.

You see life through the lens of your self-concept.

Your self-image colors everything you see in life. It is the lens through which you look at all of life. Therefore, it's important to be aware of how you feel and think about yourself. A cartoon I have in my office illustrates this very well. It shows a fellow looking in a mirror and asking his reflection a very important question: "Are you 'fer' me or 'ag'in' me today?"

Very often, your best friend or worst enemy is the person you see when you look in the mirror. If someone were to ask you what you thought of the person you see reflected when you look into a mirror, what would you say?

Remember, the image you have formed of yourself over the years has become the lens through which you look at life. None of us sees life as it really is. We see it the way it looks through the lens of our self-image. In whatever way your view of yourself is distorted, your view of life is warped.

"You'll find people like that wherever you go."

In earlier days of our history, travelers were dependent on ferry boats to get them across our nation's rivers. The story is told of a wise old ferry boat captain who made it a practice to talk to his passengers as he ferried them back and forth across the river.

On one side he struck up a conversation with a woman who seemed to be upset. She said, "You know, sir, I have never been so glad to get away from a place in all my life as I am to leave here. People here are downright mean. They butter you up to your face, but behind your back they cut you up in little pieces and spit you out. I'm leaving some of the most hateful people I've ever known."

"Yes, ma'am," agreed the old ferry boat captain. "You'll find people like that wherever you go."

When he picked up his load of passengers from the other side of the river, he began to talk to another lady. She was weeping. "You know, sir, it breaks my heart to leave this place. I've never been around more loving people. I've made so many wonderful friends here, it's like I'm leaving a big piece of my heart in this place."

"Yes, ma'am," the wise old ferry boat captain responded. "You'll find people like that wherever you go."

35

As you can see, each of these women looked at life through her own unique lens. Each made a very different impression on the old ferry boat captain. The particular impression each woman made was the result of her unique view of life. This came from the way each saw herself. The wise old captain knew each woman would continue to see people—wherever she went—the way she had seen them in the place from which she had come.

Each of us makes a unique impression on others.

Periodically, we need to pause and ask ourselves what kind of impression we are leaving on others. If we are not pleased with our answer, we can do something about it. We can change the way we see ourselves and others by changing the lens through which we look at life.

You were not born with the view of life you presently hold. This is something you learned once you got here. Nor have you always felt about life the way you do today. Through the years, your feelings about life have grown out of the way you have learned to see yourself.

Anything we learn we can modify and change—for better or for worse—even the way we see ourselves. So, if you are uncomfortable with the way you see yourself, then thank God you can do something about it. *You can change the lens through which you look at life.* That's what this chapter is all about!

In learning how you can change your view of life, we will be considering these important questions on self-image: What are we referring to when we speak of our self-image? Why is our self-image so important? Where do we get our self-image? If we don't like the one we have, how do we go about changing it?

What is a person's self-image?

Your self-image is a reflection of how you believe other people see you. This does not mean other people actually see you this way. It only means this is the way you *believe* other people see you. In other words, your self-image does not consist of who you think you are. It consists of *who you think other people think you are.*

Initially, your perception of how you are viewed by your parents determines how you see yourself. This is not necessarily the way your parents actually viewed you; rather, it is how you believed they viewed you. Once you start to school, the way you believe your peers and other significant adults view you also plays an important role in determining your self-image.

Sharpening the definition of your self-image.

Your self-image consists of what you have come to believe to be honest and true about yourself. Unfortunately, if you were to ask many people, "What do you believe to be honest and true about yourself," they couldn't tell you. They are so anxious and confused about life in general that their views of themselves are very uncertain and poorly defined. They tend to believe whatever the person they are with at the moment says is true about them.

A simple way to assess your self-image is to ask yourself, "How do I feel about the person I'm with when I'm alone?" To be more specific, you may want to write the following sentence stem ten times and fill in the blanks:

"I am a person who _____."

By filling in the blanks, you will discover ten things that you believe to be important and true about yourself. Why not take time to do that now? As you continue with the chapter, you will discover how these statements color your view of yourself, color your view of God, and affect the way you believe God sees you.

These statements define the lens through which you look at life. That is why your self-image is so very important. Everything you experience in life is filtered through it. *Even your view of God is filtered through the way you see yourself.* In fact, it is difficult—if not impossible—for you to have a healthy view of God *without* having a healthy view of yourself. And the reverse is also true. It is difficult—if not impossible—for you to have an *unhealthy* view of God without having an *unhealthy* view of yourself. We'll talk more about this a little later.

Learn the secret of being a positive person!

Your view of life in general is a product of your self-image. The more positively you see yourself, the more optimistic your view of life will tend to be. The more negatively you see yourself, the more pessimistic your view of life will tend to be. This is part of what Paul refers to in 1 Corinthians 13:12 (KJV), where he writes, *"Now we see through a glass darkly."*

Our fallen nature makes it impossible for us to see life as God intended when He made us in His image. Sin distorts our view. Our limited knowledge and experience further warp our vision of reality. Your self-image either adds clarity or brings confusion to your view of life. This is why it is so important.

How is your self-image formed?

The major components of your self-image are:

1. The family environment in which you are raised.
2. The way you choose to respond to that environment.

You were not born with any preconceived ideas about yourself. And yet, none of us can remember a time when we didn't have definite ideas about ourselves. As you can see, the acquisition of a self-image predates memory. The view you have of yourself has grown out of the complex interactions between you and members of your family during the first three to five years of your life.

For example, your self-image may be affected by the way your parents felt about your arrival. After all, the arrival of a child is not always planned or welcomed. Because we are so tiny and fragile when we come into the world, it is important that the people to whom we are born be *pleased* with our arrival even if

38

they didn't *plan for it*—we are totally dependent upon them for our survival. The way parents feel about a baby's birth will be communicated to the child through subtle nuances of touch, sight, and sound during the times when they feed, bathe, and change the child.

There are also many other issues in those preverbal years that have an important bearing on your self-image: How often were you held and hugged? How gently or abruptly were you weaned? How patiently or impatiently were you toilet-trained? How did your parents react when they saw you fondle your genitals as an infant? How frequently were you yelled at and/or spanked? How often were you commended? How often were you criticized? How fairly or unfairly were you disciplined? How much freedom were you given? How much responsibility were you expected to assume? How many times did your family move?

None of these things should be viewed as solely determining your self-image. However, any of them may have had a more or less important bearing on the way you learned to feel about yourself by the time you were old enough to talk.

Remember, no child is born with an image of himself or herself. But by the time each of us starts school, the ways we have learned to feel and think about ourselves are so obvious that any observant teacher readily recognizes them. Once your self-image is formed, it tends to be *stable over time* and *highly resistant to change.*

Where did you wind up in the parade?

Your self-image is also affected by such things as how many brothers and sisters you have, how many children were already in the family when you came along, and how many more came after you. Although each person reacts to his or her birth order in a unique way, there are generalizations which can provide some insight as to how birth order positions affect us.

39

The first child.

For example, some couples have been waiting for years for their first child to be born so they could correct all the parenting mistakes they believe their parents made with them. This first child is the one many parents try to make perfect. However, the first child also has several advantages.

Those who occupy this position have both parents' full and undivided attention. They do not have to share their parents' love and attention with anyone else until another child is born. Nor do they have to share their toys. And parents have time to give the first child more individual attention during those important early months of learning than their other children will receive.

On the other hand, greater parental demands are made on the first child than on subsequent children. After all, parents reason, they are older and should know more than the other children. Therefore, parents are often more critical of their first child. However, first children are also likely to receive more parental praise than later children.

As a result of these unique factors, first children tend to be very responsible, extremely conscientious, highly productive people. They are usually the family's first free babysitter. This may help to explain why some oldest children grow up to be a bit bossy. They are also—quite often—prone to guilt and depression.

The baby.

The baby of the family holds a very interesting position as well. Usually, older children are expected to make special allowances for the baby. Families take special care of the baby. So, the baby of the family often grows up expecting others to take care of him or her. The longer the family has been without a baby before the last baby is born, the more most family members tend to cater to that baby.

Parents should see that these children have plenty of experiences with other children their age. This will provide the experiences such a child needs in order to learn the normal "give and take" one usually acquires from brothers and sisters near their age. This will also help the youngest child learn to be less self-centered and better able to share with others.

Because of all the love and attention they are likely to receive, the baby of the family is seldom insecure. They may, however, go through life wanting to be cared for by others.

The middle child.

The middle child holds the "good news/bad news" position in the family, lacking the attention given to the first child and the baby of the family. However, when there are only three children in the family, the middle child has an enviable opportunity to compete with his or her siblings for parental love and attention. If the middle child succeeds in getting the needed attention, he or she has probably mastered a skill that our society rewards handsomely—competition.

Children raised in the middle positions of a large family are most likely to suffer from a negative self-image. They are not close enough to the front or back of the line to get the love and attention they need. Often, therefore, they grow up more anxiety- and depression-prone than their brothers and sisters who are close one end or the other of the sibling parade.

How did you know that your parents loved each other?

Another important factor in your self-image is the amount of love and affection you received while you were growing up. That's why any adult reaching out to one of our counselors for help is going to be asked, "As a child, how did you know your parents loved each other?"

An adult with fond memories of family affection is more likely to have a positive self-image than one raised in a family

41

lacking in affection. So, I'm always glad when I get the kind of response to that question one man who was raised in the south gave me. He said, "I knew my mom and dad loved each other because they were always a lovin' on one another." Children brought up in homes where there is plenty of affection are to be envied.

Usually, when we ask people about how they knew their parents loved each other, there is a long pause as they begin to reflect. Finally, we are likely to hear something like, "Well, there wasn't much of a display of affection in our home. I seldom heard my parents say they loved each other. So, I guess I knew they did because they stayed together."

Another important question!

After we learn how they knew their parents loved each other, we ask a second important question, "How did you know they loved you?" People who have the most scarred and distorted images of themselves have a difficult time recalling how they knew their dad and mom loved them. As children, they were seldom held, hugged, kissed, or told they were loved.

If you can remember having healthy thoughts and feelings about yourself as a child, thank God for your parents. And if your parents are still alive, call them or write to them often to thank them for the good start in life they gave you.

Of course, birth order and the amount of affection in the family are just two of many variables that make up the matrix of one's self-image. More important than these factors alone is how you choose to perceive and react to them.

Exert your control where it counts.

We have little or no control over the choices others make in determining our environment. However, we do have control over how we choose to respond to that environment.

Over the years, I have seen people from very similar environments turn out very differently in life. Some have been raised in supportive environments and still have chosen to see themselves in a very negative way. Others have grown up in horribly destructive environments and managed to preserve a very positive view of themselves.

When we are growing up, we find many things about our lives beyond our control. However, as adults, none of us live with the actual events. We live with our memories of those events. And—as we'll see later—thank God, memories can be edited.

Your self-image is your key to happiness.

Your happiness is largely determined by how you feel and think about yourself—and how you choose to feel and think about what happens to you in life. Both of these affect and are affected by your self-image, the lens through which you look at life. Solomon said it well: *"As he thinketh in his heart, so is he"* (Proverbs 23:7, KJV).

Jesus spoke of this great truth in Matthew 12:34,35 (KJV):

"... For out of the abundance of the heart the mouth speaketh. A good man out of the good treasure of the heart bringeth forth good things: and an evil man out of the evil treasure bringeth forth evil things."

What do these verses mean? Jesus is simply explaining that you can know much about the content of people's hearts from listening to their conversation. This is also a basic tenet of psychology.

What does your conversation tell others?

When you listen to a person talk, that person is telling you what is in his or her heart. A person is unable to keep still about what is being stored up in the heart. Sooner or later, whatever the heart is full of will surface in conversation.

43

I encourage you to begin to listen to yourself when you talk to others. What are your favorite topics of conversation? How broadly conversant are you with the issues of the day? Is there depth to your conversation or do you major in trivia? When you talk about people, do you generally tend to build them up or do you tear them down? As you analyze your philosophy of life from your conversation, is it optimistic or pessimistic?

How do you talk to yourself?

As important as it is for you to be aware of your conversation with others, it is even more important to tune in to what you say when you talk to yourself. What you choose to say to other people is just a sample of what you keep telling yourself. And the way you talk to yourself both *grows out of* and *contributes to* your self-image.

If you've grown up with the idea that others are smarter than you, emotionally stronger than you, and more likable than you, then you are likely to feel inferior and insecure much of the time. This view of yourself has grown out of your perceptions of other people's view of you. And as long as you express this view to yourself, it will be reflected in your conversations with others.

Your happiness or unhappiness flows out of how you choose to talk to yourself about your life's relationships and events. When I have tried to assure people that they could see themselves and life much more positively, I've had many tell me, "But you just don't know what my family was like when I was growing up."

I usually respond to those remarks with, "What has happened to us in life is not nearly as important to our happiness as the way we choose to respond to what has happened. After all, none of us lives with just the events of his or her life. We live with the stories we tell ourselves about the events of our lives."

These stories we tell ourselves about our lives become our memories of life. Neither the events of our lives nor the facts which describe them can be changed. However, our memories can be edited. What a redemptive thought!

None of us grows up in ideal circumstances. One of the big deceptions of our fallen minds is the belief that if we had another person's circumstances we would be happier. However, even if we had someone else's circumstances, we would still *interpret them* in our own way. *Our way of interpreting life's circumstances is what needs to change.*

"He can't swim, can he?"

As an example, let me tell you a story I once heard about a duck hunter who bought a dog to retrieve his game for him. The first time he took the dog hunting, no one else was with him. On his first shot, a duck fell into the water. Immediately, the dog walked out *on* the water, picked up the duck in his mouth, and returned it to his master.

The man couldn't believe his own eyes. However, the same thing happened three more times before the day was over. As he stowed his game and his gear in the van, he thought to himself, "I could *never* tell anybody about this. No one would believe me. They'd think I was crazy." So he made arrangements to take a hunting buddy with him the next time.

The day went like it had gone when he was alone. Every time he or his buddy would shoot a duck, his dog would walk out on the water, pick it up, and bring it back to them. The friend gave no indication that he noticed anything different about this dog. Finally, they were packing their game and gear back into the van. The dog's proud owner couldn't tolerate his friend's silence any longer. He turned to his friend and asked, "Did you notice anything unusual about my dog today?"

"Yeah," his friend replied. "He can't swim!"

You view your own circumstances and those of others in your own way. Circumstances don't determine your happiness. It is the way you choose to view them and talk to yourself about them which becomes critical to your happiness.

Eleanor Roosevelt is credited with saying, "Nobody can make me feel inferior without my permission." To paraphrase her observation, we could as easily say, "Nobody can make me feel *any way at all* without my permission." Think about it! Our feelings are our chosen reactions to life's events.

The way you see it is the way it is for you.

A person with a *negative* self-image can be in the most positive circumstances possible and not find anything to be encouraged about. On the other hand, a person with a *positive* self-image can weather some very severe storms in life without being done in by them.

Everyone's "sky" has its dark clouds.

People who don't know me often say to me, "You can say all that about interpreting circumstances positively because life has been kind to you. If you knew the terrible circumstances in which I grew up, you'd know why I feel this way."

I suppose it's easy for us to assume that life has treated other people better than it has us, especially if we don't know them. So, let me tell you something about my early life.

My mother was married the first time when she was fifteen. Her husband brutalized her, so she divorced him. When she was eighteen, she married my father. When she was nineteen, they were expecting me. Thirteen days after she gave birth to me, she died. My birth killed my mother.

Now, my aunt had been married and was left a widow with a little girl. When my father needed somebody to take care of me and she needed help taking care of her little girl, the two of them got married. Six years later, they had a girl of their own. I grew up in a home where it was, "your kid, my kid, and our kid."

This is just a little peek into the pages of my life, but I hope it helps you see that pain and trouble come to everyone. No one's skies are always sunny. We all have storms. It's how you choose to talk to yourself during these storms that determines— to a great extent—how sunny or dark your sky will be.

No one else can talk to you fast enough to change you.

You may ask, "Why is the way I talk to myself so important?" It's because no other person can talk to you as fast as you talk to yourself. A minister or public speaker can only talk to you at the rate of about *two to three hundred* words per minute. But your mind is so amazing that it allows you to talk to yourself in thought at speeds of *three to four thousand* words per minute.

This is why it is so easy for your thoughts to stray when you are bored. If a speaker can hold your attention, your mind will stay on the subject. But if it gets a little boring, your mind takes you on a dozen side trips into yesterday or tomorrow.

Remember, others can only talk to you at the rate of two to three hundred words per minute. Your parents cannot talk to you faster than that. Neither can a friend or your mate. Basically, *this is why no one else can make you happy.*

This is why I advise anyone who is married to a person who is miserable not to try to make that person happy. Trying to make a miserable person happy is a good way to lose your own happiness. Remember, for every hundred words you can use to bring your mate out of his misery, his own internal speech habits will have presented him with a thousand words to convince him that life is still as miserable as he thinks it is. You're outnumbered ten words to one before you start. You may as well save your breath to cool your soup!

Only you can change your feelings.

God knows that your happiness is too important an issue for Him to put in anyone's hands but yours—and His. It is unfair for any of us to expect someone else to change the way we feel about ourself or life. Nor do I want anyone else determining whether I'm going to be happy. I want that freedom and responsibility right in my own grasp and God's.

If in the process of growing up you received a wholesome self-image through which to view life, then you have no need to change your self-image. However, many of us had parents who were very preoccupied with their own pain when we came into their lives. They were unaware of how we were learning to feel and think about ourselves as we were growing up. They wouldn't have intentionally given us a miserable way of looking at life or a negative way of seeing ourselves for anything in the world. But our arrival came when they were so immersed in the hurts from their past and pressures from their present that they didn't understand how we were learning to look at life. Provision for our emotional comfort was lost in concern over their own pain.

Can a believer who has a damaged self-image change the way he feels and thinks about himself? Yes, thank God, he can. *This is what being born again is all about.* In 2 Corinthians 3:17,18, Paul tells us that we can all be changed more and more into the image of Christ. Just as we receive our natural self-image from the earthly parents to whom we are born, we have an opportunity, once we have been regenerated, to be recreated in the image of our heavenly Father.

Regeneration makes recreation possible—not inevitable.

Every born-again person has the opportunity to become "new" in Jesus. What he does with the opportunity is up to him.

"Yet to all who received him, to those who believed in his name, he gave the right to become children of God— children born not of natural descent, nor of human decision or a husband's will, but born of God."
(John 1:12,13, NIV)

For many of us, achieving this goal requires the transformation of the badly damaged self-image we bring with us into God's kingdom. Directions from God's Word and the dynamics of His Spirit are at our disposal in our pursuit of this goal. However, we have to take the initiative and *apply* these resources if our view of ourself is going to be changed.

How can you go about changing your self-image?

Many believers expect this to happen magically at the instant of conversion, with little or no personal effort. Although the miracle of God's grace is an essential dynamic in any such transformation, the believer must also put forth conscious and deliberate effort in the process. God doesn't require you to do what you can't, but *He does expect you to do what you can.*

Here are some practical steps for changing your self-image.

1.   See yourself as a person God loves very much.

Certainly, there is nothing about the fallen nature of the human race that makes us lovable. Even a casual look at our collective history reveals us to be self-destructive and detestable. Our personal histories justify the same conclusion. However, through His grace, God has chosen to love us. He wants us to see ourselves as children *dearly loved* by their heavenly Father.

This is something new for some believers. It's amazing to see how many Christians find it difficult to think of themselves as dearly loved by God.

Some Christians see themselves in such a negative way as to make receiving a simple compliment difficult. How easy is it for you to *accept a compliment?* When someone says to you, "Oh, you look so nice tonight," do you find it necessary to tell them you bought your dress on sale or got your suit at a discount? Are you likely to respond to a compliment with an apology? Is it difficult for you to simply say, "Thank you, I appreciate that"?

49

How easy is it for you to *receive expressions of love* from other people? Can you see why they would love you? Do you see yourself as someone God loves very much? Your heavenly Father *wants* you to see yourself this way.

Regardless of how you may feel your earthly parents viewed you, when you look at the cross, there should never be any doubt about how your heavenly Father feels about you. Remember, Calvary does not tell you how much God loves you. Calvary only tells you how much God loves His enemies. Romans 5:6-8 (KJV) says:

> *"For when we were yet without strength, in due time Christ died for the ungodly. For scarcely for a righteous man will one die: yet peradventure for a good man some would even dare to die. But God commendeth his love toward us, in that, while we were yet sinners, Christ died for us."*

God loves His children "much more."

"Well," you may say, "If God loves His *enemies* that much, how much does He love His *children?*" Perhaps you will only begin to understand how much God loves you as His child when you visualize above the cross the words, *"Much more."* Romans 5:9,10 (KJV) says:

> *"Much more, then, being now justified by his blood, we shall be saved from wrath through him. For if, when we were enemies, we were reconciled to God by the death of his Son, much more, being reconciled, we shall be saved by his life."*

If you want to remember how much God loves you as His child, I would suggest that you make a cross somewhere in the flyleaf of your Bible. Above that cross write the question, "How much does God love me?" Then write the answer: "God loves me much more!"

How much does God love me?
" Much more! "

Can you fathom that? God loves you and me more than Calvary can express. That's the way your heavenly Father wants you to see yourself. He wants you to know how much you are loved.

2.   Realize you are very valuable to God.

One of the common afflictions I see believers suffering from is a very low sense of self-worth. Many believers simply do not understand the difference between being unworthy and being worthless. They make a mental equation of the two words. To them, being unworthy = being worthless.

These terms are not synonymous. To be unworthy is not equal to being worthless. None of us can ever be worthy of the price our heavenly Father paid for us. How could we ever be proud enough to think we "deserve" the blood of Christ? However, if our heavenly Father had not imputed that much worth to us, He would never have paid such a price for us.

Worth is established by the amount one is willing to pay for something. It is actually set in the marketplace. When you and I were sold under sin, our heavenly Father redeemed us—not with corruptible things such as silver or gold, but with the precious blood of Christ.

"For God so loved the world, that he gave his only begotten Son, that whosoever believeth in him should not perish but have everlasting life" (John 3:16, KJV).

"Forasmuch as ye know that ye were not redeemed with corruptible things, as silver and gold, from your vain conversation [way of life] received by tradition from your fathers; but with the precious blood of Christ, as of a lamb without blemish and without spot."

(1 Peter 1:18,19, KJV)

"Do you not know that your body is a temple of the Holy Spirit, who is in you, whom you have received from God? You are not your own; you were bought at a price. Therefore honor God with your body."

(1 Corinthians 6:19,20, NIV)

We can never be worthy of that price. But the fact that Christ paid it makes us know God does not consider us worthless. You and I are of great worth to God.

In His challenge to His disciples, Jesus declared each human being to be worth more than the total material wealth of the whole world. In Mark 8:36 (KJV), He said, *"For what shall it profit a man, if he shall gain the whole world, and lose his own soul?"*

Were it possible for one man to pursue and possess the wealth of the whole world, and were he to lose himself in the process, Jesus declares that what he would lose (himself) would be worth more than what he would gain in material possessions.

You may be thinking, "But I remember a Scripture that says when we've done everything we ought to do, we should consider ourselves unprofitable servants (see Luke 17:10, KJV). That's true. We're still unprofitable—but not worthless!

Remember, profit is an economic term. It refers to the amount returned to the investor in excess of the amount of his investment. How can you and I return to God an amount in excess of the price He paid to redeem us? That is impossible. If I did everything I could possibly do to repay my heavenly Father for the price of my redemption, I still would be unprofitable.

Jesus did not tell that parable to make us feel worthless. He simply wanted us to know that Calvary was no business deal for our heavenly Father. It was a love affair, and love never looks for profit!

Your heavenly Father loves you very much. He also considers you to be a valuable person. Begin to say that to yourself over and over again: "God loves me very much. I am very valuable to Him."

3.   Think of yourself as a forgivable person.

Many believers suffer needless pain from unhealthy guilt, all the while unconsciously assuming there is some virtue in continuing to suffer for their own sins. Friend, it was Christ's sufferings which atoned for our sins, not our own. And when He suffered, He not only suffered enough for my sins and your sins, He suffered enough for the sins of the whole world. So there is no virtue to be gained in continuing to suffer for our own sins. Jesus suffered enough.

You *may* have to live with the *natural consequences* of some previous sin. But it is *never* God's will for you to suffer continued *guilt* for that sin. For example, a person may drive his automobile under the influence of alcohol and lose a limb in an accident. Although he will never regain his limb, God doesn't want him to suffer additionally crippling guilt the rest of his life because of what he did.

Any sin you sincerely confess, God will forgive.

Satan, as the accuser of the believer, puts condemning thoughts into our minds. He may suggest that what you did at some point in your past is too wicked for even God to forgive. But remember, he's a liar. God's Word says:

53

"If we confess our sins, he is faithful and just to forgive us our sins, and to cleanse us from all unrighteousness."

(1 John 1:9, KJV)

Anything I am honest enough to confess, God is faithful enough to forgive. If you have confessed it to Christ, He has forgiven it. Now, practice saying to yourself, "I am a forgiven person." Say it to yourself over and over again until every bit of guilt from your past is gone . . . under the blood of Christ . . . in the past . . . never to be remembered against you again.

"I, even I, am he who blots out your transgressions for my own sake, and remembers your sins no more."

(Isaiah 43:25, NIV)

4.   See yourself as a changeable person.

At times, the process of change may require us to "pray through" some of our old hurts. This form of creative prayer is a simple self-help technique I have discovered to be effective in my own life and have used to help many others achieve desired changes.

For example, I have already shared with you the fact that my birth killed my mother. As I grew up, the way I interpreted that fact changed several times. When I was four, I wondered why I couldn't have a mommy out of whose "tummy" I came. As an ornery ten- or eleven-year-old, I was putting those facts together to say, "The reason I get into so much trouble is that I'm a bad kid. After all, my birth killed my mother."

As a teenager, after I became a Christian, I became more and more aware of an increasing desire to go to my mother's grave. I hadn't been there in years. The first few times I went, I wept to think that a nineteen-year-old young woman had died to give me life, but I still left with that hurt in me.

Then, on one particular visit when I was nineteen years old, as I stood there thinking about how young my mother had been

54

when she died, the Holy Spirit inspired this thought in my mind: "Not only did *Jesus* die for you, but your *mother* died for you. How valuable your life must be. See that you make it count for something."

My mother's death was still the result of my birth. I couldn't change the events. But my *memories* could be edited! Now I was saying that somehow her death added to the worth of my life and I needed to make my life count for something. I had not changed the *events* of my life—God had helped me discover a less painful way of *remembering those events.* What He did for me, I have seen Him do for many others.

Through creative prayer, God can help you edit painful parts of your past and create an understanding you can more easily live with. Since people sometimes express intense feelings when they are "praying through" their old hurts, I encourage them to do this when they are alone. Here are the four steps in the process:

1.   Talk to God honestly about what hurts you.

Great men and women of Scripture have always found the courage to do this and so can you. It isn't easy, but it is the only way prayer can bring you the practical help you need when life is hurting you.

Look at the way Jacob resolved the issues of guilt and fear he had carried for years against Esau. He was a whole night in prayer coming to terms with those feelings (Genesis 32). Remember David's honesty when he bared his heart to God over what went on between him and Bathsheba (Psalm 51). And don't forget the bitter tears Peter shed over his denial of Christ (Matthew 26:75).

Whatever the issues may be in your life that are keeping you from seeing yourself the way God sees you in Christ, determine to talk to God honestly about them.

2.   Express your feelings about your hurts to God.

As you begin to talk honestly to God about what hurts you, the feelings associated with those hurts will probably surface. Express those feelings.

You may want to weep or express intensely angry feelings to God. David did. In Psalm 58:6, he begged God to break the teeth of his enemies. In Psalm 59:13-15 (KJV), he prayed concerning his enemies:

> *"Consume them in wrath, consume them, that they may not be: and let them know that God ruleth in Jacob unto the ends of the earth . . . And at evening, let them return: and let them make a noise like a dog, and go 'round about the city. Let them wander up and down for meat."*

You may be thinking, "But I don't want God to know I feel that way about my enemies." Think how ridiculous that is! If those feelings are there, how can you hide them from God?

Even though you would never *act out* those feelings, carrying them around buried inside of you can keep you from enjoying life. You need to get your feelings out in the presence of someone who will keep them confidential and someone you can trust with them. You need to express them to *God.*

As you pour your feelings out to God in a time of private prayer, you eventually bare your soul. Everything bottled up inside you gets emptied out before the Lord. The burden of your heart is lifted. You are now ready for the third step in the process of praying through your hurts:

3.   Meditate for a new meaning from your old hurts.

You can never *think* differently about your old hurts until you *feel* differently about them. However, once you've emptied out your old feelings before God, you are in a position for Him to comfort you and show you a new way to look at your old hurts.

Just as God helped David turn loose of his hatred and bitterness toward those who had hurt him, the Lord will help you surrender your hurts and will suggest to your mind new, more constructive ways of looking at them as you quietly meditate before Him. Remember David's prayer in Psalm 139:23,24 (KJV):

"Search me, O God, and know my heart: try me, and know my thoughts: and see if there be any wicked way in me, and lead me in the way everlasting."

Options for new meanings to old hurts come in a variety of forms, from a variety of sources. You may find them in the words of a favorite hymn or a stirring sermon; you may find Bible stories and parables coming to mind. Options may also come from the heart of a trusted friend. Consider all of the possibilities in light of tomorrow, as well as today. Which is best for you in the long run? Over time, as you think and meditate on all the possible options open to you, one will stand out from the others as God's gift to you—the new way He's given you to look at an old hurt.

4.   Praise God for the new meaning He gives you!

As God gives you the ability to see your old hurt in a new and less painful way, thank Him and praise Him for it. Repeat the new meaning several times in praise and prayer so that when in the future Satan suggests the old meaning in your thoughts again, you will have learned the new one so well and will have embedded it so deeply in your mind that the old one will have no more grip on you.

Don't expect all of this to happen in just one session of creative prayer. It may happen that way; however, it is more likely to require several times of prayer to bring the healing you need. After all, we have not arrived at this point of intense emotional pain in just minutes ... and we're not likely to become completely different in just minutes. We have become the way we are through a *process.* And, most likely, it will require a *process* to change us. But that process has to start sometime and someplace. So, why not let it be *this time and this place?*

It doesn't matter how old you are. Your future can be different from and better than your past. Look at Grandma Moses. She was past retirement age when she discovered her genius for painting. And Colonel Sanders was old enough to live on Social Security before he became a millionaire.

You don't have to stay the way you are. Within each of us there is an undiscovered world of divine potential. Jesus wants to put you in touch with that potential He has placed in you so that you can know exciting change in Him!

God doesn't want you to remain crippled by the pain of your past. He has more wholesome ways for you to view those things. And, He wants you to be able to see yourself as He sees you: someone He loves, values, forgives, and wants very much to change.

The next time you look in a mirror, say to yourself: "I'm looking at someone God loves. Someone God says is valuable. Someone who has been totally forgiven. I'm looking at someone who is becoming more and more like my heavenly Father."

When we begin to see ourselves as God sees us in Jesus, then the world begins to see Jesus in us. Then we are well on our way to defeating the self-consciousness, fears, and anxieties which cripple so many believers. In the next chapter, we will be taking a closer look at some practical ways of dealing with those would-be giants who threaten to keep us from our Promised Land.

Chapter 3

"Nothing to Fear but Fear Itself"

Facing the Fears of Life

On March 4, 1933, during some of the darkest days of the Great Depression, President Franklin Delano Roosevelt said in his first inaugural address, *"The only thing we have to fear is fear itself."* His brave words inspired courage in the American people as they endured the fourth year of an economic depression that seemed to stretch endlessly into the future.

Panic had rocked Wall Street. Family fortunes had vanished overnight. Many who could not face the loss of their wealth had committed suicide. More than 13 million Americans were unemployed—over 25 percent of the labor force! Many were on the verge of starvation. Thousands lived in tent cities, in cardboard shacks, and on the streets. The country was on the brink of anarchy and revolution.

The president knew fear's destructive power was our nation's greatest enemy. From his own battle with polio, he had learned the creative power of hope and courage. So, he

59

challenged the American people to rise above their fears—and they did! For six more long years, most Americans did without many of the bare necessities of life, but somehow they managed to live above their fears and look toward the better day that must surely come.

Today, God challenges us to live above fear—to deny it a destructive reign in our lives. In this chapter, we will examine some Biblical ways of doing this.

Everyone knows what it is to be afraid.

Fear and anxiety are more of a problem for some than for others. However, no human being lives totally free from fear. Fear was the immediate consequence of Adam's fall. In Genesis 3:18 (NIV) we read:

> *"Then the man and his wife heard the sound of the LORD God as he was walking in the garden in the cool of the day, and they hid from the LORD God among the trees of the garden. But the LORD God called to the man, 'Where are you?' He answered, 'I heard you in the garden, and I was afraid because I was naked; so I hid.'"*

Ever since that fateful moment, fear is the first emotion a human being experiences. Thomas Hobbes said, "Myself and fear were born twins." None of us can remember a time in life when we began to fear. Our proneness to fear precedes our memory.

Some fears are healthy, but many are unnecessary.

Often, good Christians allow themselves to be worried out of many of the good things in life God intends for them to enjoy. Recall the exercise already mentioned, where people were asked to write on the front of a sheet of paper all the things they had worried about during the past year . . . then they were asked to turn the paper over and write on the back all of those things about which they had worried that actually happened.

Even though the list on the back was very short, this was not enough to convince them that worrying didn't help. Inevitably, some people replied, "But think of all those things that *might have happened* if I hadn't worried about them!"

Fear is tormenting!

The Apostle John records what we all have discovered by experience: *"Fear hath torment"* (1 John 4:18, KJV). I vividly recall the fear that gripped me in the middle of the night several years ago. I awakened, looked out the upstairs bedroom window, and saw someone apparently trying to steal our car. I was so frightened by what I saw that when I called the police to report the suspected theft I began to whisper to them over the phone. The man who was taking the information had to assure me that if I would keep the lights off in the house it was perfectly safe for me to talk loud enough to be heard over the phone. Only then was I able to speak up so that he could hear me.

Fear tends to paralyze and blind!

The torment that accompanies fear threatens to render us powerless. Often, when it strikes we cannot think clearly or act wisely. This is undoubtedly one of the reasons Jesus so often encouraged His disciples not to be afraid. Fear blinds us to alternatives in problem-solving and options for decision-making which otherwise would be obvious to us.

As we learn to become aware of the Lord's presence in our daily lives, we trust Him more in times when we are afraid. From the awareness of His presence we draw the courage to respond to life in wiser, more creative ways. Sometimes life confronts us with the need for this kind of mature trust in God before we have had time or opportunity to develop it.

Recently, I sat with a pregnant teenager. She and the teenage young man involved had met at church. She was a believer, but he made no profession of faith. They had gone together for several months. He had convinced her that he loved her dearly and wanted to marry her. However, when she told him she was pregnant, he angrily rejected her. He wouldn't even talk to her over the phone for several weeks.

By the time she talked to me, she had already seen her pastor, who had helped her confess the sin of her sexual misbehavior to the Lord. She had found the forgiveness she needed to deal with the overwhelming guilt such a situation provokes. God gave her the courage to resist the pressure her boyfriend and his family had put on her to have an abortion.

When she saw me, she was struggling with the three remaining options. None of them seemed to be good ones. She was trying to determine which of them would be the least destructive. Should she place the baby for adoption through a Christian child-placement agency? If so, would the adoptive parents be able to give the baby as much love and as many opportunities in life as she could? Would they be able to offer more? What effect would being adopted have on her child's future? How could she live, knowing she had a child growing up in someone else's home?

Should she keep the baby and raise it by herself? Her parents would help her, but she would have to bear the primary responsibility. Could she count on regular support payments from the child's natural father? Could she live on what she could get from welfare? How fair was it to expect her parents to meet the expenses of this child out of their limited budget? What kind of opportunities could she give this child as a single parent? Would any other man want to marry her if she brought this child into the marriage?

Should she marry the child's father? He has told her he will marry her, but he doesn't want to do that until after the baby is born. What if she does marry him? He's not a believer. How long could the marriage be expected to last? Having suffered the rejection, embarrassment, and guilt of being single and pregnant, must she also assume the high risk of being divorced and a single parent before she reaches age 30?

What are the chances that a teenager can overcome the fear and anxiety of such a moment to adequately consider questions like these? It is extremely difficult for any person, regardless of age, to see the wisest option in such a pressure-packed situation. Even if this young woman could have seen her wisest option, how likely is it that she could have found the courage to act on it without the strength of her faith?

Christians are never alone in their fears.

The kind of insight and courage we need in such frightening and anxious moments can only come when we are willing to focus on God's presence with us. Only then can He help us discover His will *in spite of* our fears.

After having thoroughly discussed each of these options with this young lady, I said to her, "I can certainly understand why you feel overwhelmed by the fear and anxiety of the moment. Any normal person in your place would feel the same way. That someone so young should have to make such an awesome decision is tragic and regrettable. However, you are a Christian. And God knows the wisest way for you to deal with this dilemma. Even though you are in this situation because of your own misbehavior and carelessness, don't add to your pain by assuming that God has forsaken you. He hasn't. And He won't. If you will open your mind and spirit to Him, He will help you discern which of the options we've discussed is best for you. You can trust Him to guide you."

In my prayer with her, I asked God to make His presence real to her. I asked Him to help her overcome her fear and anxiety, rise above the pressure of the moment, and deny the insistence of her own desires. I prayed that in the following days she would be willing to consider any one of the three options to be God's will for her. I asked God to consistently and persistently surface in her mind the option which represented His best choice for her.

As she left my office, she thanked me for making her aware of the ways in which her fear and anxiety could blind her. She expressed appreciation to me for helping her define and think through each of her options. She assured me that she never was more aware of her need of the Lord and expressed a determination to find and do His will. Learning to trust the Lord for wisdom in such a frightening moment is a valuable lesson in crisis management that can serve one well throughout life.

Many crippling fears are irrational.

On the other hand, through the years, I have seen men and women whose lives have been paralyzed by fears which were not so easily understood. It's one thing to be frightened of circumstances which would scare anyone. It is another thing for your life to be paralyzed by unreasonable fears.

For example, some people are so fearful of germs that they are gripped by an overwhelming compulsion to wash their hands. Of course, I'm not talking about the normal needs for cleanliness we were all taught as children. Compulsive handwashing goes far beyond the scrupulous actions of a person who is extremely particular about personal cleanliness.

It is not unusual for a person who is phobic of germs to wash his or her hands a hundred times a day or more. Such an obsessive concern with germs and dirt is often an irrational diversion of one's thinking to escape dealing with one's sexuality—something such a person may consider to be far dirtier.

Other people are so fearful of social situations they cannot leave their homes by themselves. They are literally prisoners in their own homes. Some people are so crippled by this illness (agoraphobia) that they cannot be employed. When married, agoraphobics often seriously neglect their mates.

Such fears may seem ridiculous to others, but they are very real to the sufferer. Without competent professional help, these people are likely to remain victims of fear for many years. Even with professional help, recovery may be slow and difficult.

This is why it is so important to see unhealthy fears and recognize them as a devastating enemy early in life when they can be much more easily defeated. Unhealthy fears almost always can be conquered once they are identified.

In this chapter you will learn where fears come from, some ways of telling the difference between healthy and unhealthy fears, and some effective means of defeating fear . . . ways that utilize Scripture and are consistent with your faith.

Where does fear come from?

We haven't always been afraid. Before we were born, we lived in a fear-free environment. Life is never more comfortable or secure than during those last few weeks inside mother. Just think what it must have been like. Absolutely no worries! Mother's body took care of everything.

Before birth, there is no concern about food. Mother's body takes care of that. There is no need to breathe. Mother's body takes care of oxygen needs. Even elimination needs are automatically cared for by her body. In fact, nestled in the womb, comforted by the sound of mother's heartbeat, amniotic fluid even provides us our own private water bed. Can you imagine the shock when the plug is pulled and birth begins?

Birth introduces us to a fear of falling. Babies have to learn to be comfortable with movement. Every newborn baby is afraid of falling. After all, before birth, mother's body was always there for support. However, if you hold a baby in your arms and lower them rapidly, you can see the "startle reflex" spread a look of terror across the baby's face. Some adults find it amusing to see the baby extend its arms and legs in this kind of panic. However, this is a very frightening experience for the baby and should never be indulged in as a form of adult entertainment.

This fear of falling is so deeply rooted in our unconscious memory that we dream about it. How many times have you wakened in the middle of the night from a dream of falling? This feeling is so frighteningly real that jerking to avoid falling is what wakes us up.

So, birth is our introduction to fear. Suddenly and without warning, we are thrust into the world outside mother. No longer does mother supply our oxygen. Now we must find our own. No longer is our food served automatically. Now we experience hunger for the first time. And we must eat for ourselves. Our automatic waste disposal is discontinued. Now for the first time, mother has to change the diaper!

Birth drastically changes the nature of the relationship between mother and baby. Before birth, mother was uncomfortable, but she did not have to deal with the energy-demanding tasks of infant care.

Babies also fear abandonment.

Only when birth is viewed through a baby's eyes can one understand the newborn's fear of abandonment. For several weeks before birth, the baby is surrounded by a world of sound from within the mother. Her body's circulating fluids and—most important—her heartbeat are familiar sounds in the unborn's world.

The birth process forces the baby out of mother's body with very little notice. Then the baby is no longer close enough to hear those familiar sounds of mother's body. For the first time in the baby's short history, there is *no physical attachment* to mother. At times, she is no longer there. As an adult, I have a difficult time realizing how frightening such a discovery would be for a newborn.

As you can see, we have a long history with fear. It is the first emotion we experience. Before we had any fixed ideas about ourselves, we knew what it was to be afraid.

What is the difference between healthy and unhealthy fear?

Remember, all fear is painful. Even though everyone is familiar with *physical* pain, some people have to be taught that fear can cause *emotional* pain. They understand their physical pains, but they have denied the existence of emotional pain from their fears for so long they don't feel it any more.

Undoubtedly, the teenager I told you about earlier in this chapter will never experience more pain than she was experiencing during those weeks when we had our initial counseling sessions. Even though the physical pain of giving birth is intense, it could not compare with her emotional pain. And yet, I had to help her recognize and identify that emotional pain before she could experience it and deal with it. It is important to know when you are hurting emotionally!

Pain can be our friend.

Remember, pain warns us of danger. If we never experienced pain, we would be without this valuable warning. For example, if I didn't feel pain when I cut myself, I could bleed to death and never know I had been cut.

Because the brain associates pain and pleasure with places and persons, children can experience healthy fears without the risk of being hurt. They don't have to burn themselves on things that are hot in order to know that those things are hot. They can learn not to play near open stairwells. They can learn to stay away from sharp things—or, at least, to handle them with care. As adults, we learn not to be out alone in crime-ridden areas of the city. We know to avoid dark alleys. Without the emotional pain of such *healthy* fears, we couldn't survive. So let's thank God we can be afraid at *appropriate times* and in *appropriate circumstances.*

Fear also warns us of the painful consequences of disobedience. I. don't know how your parents dealt with your disobedience, and I certainly don't believe every child has to be spanked. But that's the only language some of us ever understand. I was "reared," and sometimes I can still feel it in my memories.

Fear of the consequences of disobedience also teaches us as adults to obey the law. Healthy fear teaches us healthy limits. This makes our behavior predictable and orderly, which makes an organized, functional society possible.

Holy fear.

The most important of our healthy fears is fear of the Lord. Solomon says this is the beginning of wisdom (Proverbs 9:10). Unfortunately, many people confuse *being afraid of God* with *"the fear of the LORD."* These are two very different things, as you will see shortly.

If someone is afraid of God, he has had to learn that fear. How does a person learn to be afraid of God? Sometimes, frustrated and impatient parents threaten disobedient children with God's judgment. An over-zealous evangelist may try to scare people into becoming Christians. However, neither of these approaches produces anything even remotely similar to what Solomon defined as "the fear of the LORD."

These experiences are more accurately understood as a fear of parents or a fear of preachers. No parent or preacher can put "the fear of the LORD" in you—nor would most of them want to.

You learn "the fear of the LORD" when you first experience His presence. What makes this experience the beginning of wisdom? It leaves an indelible impression on you. You never forget it. You are left with an overwhelming sense of awe and wonder. A reverence for God is forged in your mind. Continuing to experience His presence helps you order the priorities of your life more wisely. Material concerns become less important than spiritual ones.

"The fear of the LORD" does not strike terror to our hearts. It gives birth to *wisdom* in our minds. It puts a different perspective on other things we might tend to call important. We learn to desire those things that allow us to enjoy a continuing awareness of His presence. Also, we want to avoid doing those things that dull our consciousness of His presence. It gives us a better way to calculate the cost of pleasure, thus helping us choose more wisely how to spend our time and energy by reminding us of our ultimate accountability for the stewardship of life.

Religious terror!

Many believers are dominated by another kind of fear. It's not awe. It's not wonder. It's not reverence. It's sheer terror! They see God suspending them over hell by a thread. They fear the return of Christ. They fear "the mark of the beast." They fear the tribulation. They fear death.

Some even fear they have committed a sin God considers unpardonable. People who fear they have committed the unpardonable sin are pathetic. Among the hundreds of people I have seen for counseling, I have never found one whose sins were unpardonable. It is never God's will for people to suffer this kind of misery. However, because this problem is the source

69

of so much torment for so many people, I deal with it in some detail in Chapter 5.

Why are you a Christian?

Some people are Christians because they love God and enjoy being His child. Other people are Christians because they are afraid not to be. Have you met people like that? They may be on their way to heaven, but they are obviously not enjoying the trip very much.

God doesn't want you to serve Him because you are afraid of Him. He wants you to serve Him because you love Him. John says:

"There is no fear in love; but perfect love casteth out fear: because fear hath torment. He that feareth is not made perfect in love. We love him, because he first loved us."
(1 John 4:18,19, KJV)

A healthy faith should help you get the most out of life. I have *never* been able to understand the distorted idea of the Christian life being dull, drab, and uninteresting. Frequently I run into someone who implies that you can't have fun and be a Christian at the same time. I like to watch the look on such a person's face when I challenge them to show me one thing that is good for me as a human being that I can't enjoy as a Christian.

God wants me to take good care of my mind and body, but His Word does not forbid me any enjoyment of life that is consistent with my health and wholeness. As Jesus reminds us in John 10:10, it is the "thief" who comes to steal, to kill, and to destroy. God's presence opens to us a more abundant way of life.

Learn how to conquer unhealthy fear.

When we are small, our fears are often related to our physical survival. Do you remember any of your early childhood fears? I do. I can remember lying on my bed at night, watching the shadow of tree limbs mirrored on my bedroom wall as they swayed in the wind. Until I was old enough to know what I was seeing, I would imagine those shadows were all kinds of ghosts coming to get me.

Most parents have to help their small children through such painful periods of irrational fear. Such fears often surface at night. The wise parent will keep a light on in the child's bedroom. If this is not enough to provide the child with necessary comfort, it may be necessary for a few nights that a parent stay in the child's bedroom while the child drifts off to sleep. A light plus the parent's reassuring presence should help the child conquer his fear. Later, the light alone will be all the child needs. Finally, he will develop the courage to turn the light off and go to sleep on his own.

Fear of the dark, fear of snakes, fear of spiders—these are only a few of the many specific fears of children. Through our parents' love, we usually grow out of our specific fears by the time we are eight or nine years old. However, most of us come into adult life a little phobic about some things.

Some people don't like to ride elevators because they suffer such intense anxiety when confined in small spaces. This reaction is known as *claustrophobia*. It's interesting to watch what people do on elevators. Many are so uncomfortable they seldom look at others. They look at the ceiling; they look at the floor; they look at the wall. But they tolerate the discomfort for the convenience of avoiding the stairs.

Then, there's *acrophobia*—fear of high places. Once in a while, I have a little bout with that when I get on high places. I get curious about what it might feel like to jump. That feeling so frightens me that I move back from the edge or railing. This gives me a little taste of what it must be like for people who suffer crippling phobias.

71

Until they are faced, unhealthy fears will never be conquered. As adults, most of us have very few specific fears. Our fear is more general in nature. It is more anxiety-provoking than frightening. We fear talking in front of people. We fear meeting new people. We fear failing. We fear rejection.

Many of these fears are related to self-consciousness. Many Christians find self-consciousness a major source of anxiety. Later in the chapter, I will be offering some practical help for people suffering from self-consciousness. Right now, I'm going to give you four ways to deal with unhealthy fear and anxiety.

1.   Learn the value of deep-breathing exercises.

God gave you lungs for specific purposes. Sighs and deep breaths are not simply unconscious reactions to life stress. They are nature's way of relieving you of anxiety for a moment. When doing deep-breathing exercises, sit with your back against some support. Put your feet as flat on the floor as you can. Put one hand on your diaphragm. Put your other hand on top of it so you can feel yourself inhale and exhale. Slowly breathe *in* as much air as you can. Then, slowly breathe *out* as far as you can. Do this three times. Breathe in; breathe out.

After you have inhaled and exhaled three times, close your eyes and let your shoulders and head drop slightly forward. See how relaxed you feel? This simple exercise will help you *lower* your anxiety level . . . and *control* it.

You can do deep-breathing exercises on the job. When you are anxious, take advantage of your breaks to get the privacy you need and do some deep-breathing exercises. It will give you relief. Remember, it comes through divinely designed means.

2.   Apply some rational controls.

You can think yourself out of fear and anxiety. Learn to subject them to the law of averages. Ask yourself, "What are the chances that what I fear will actually happen? What are the statistical odds I'm up against?"

This may not help the habitual worrier. Often, he is like the man who stood on the street corner snapping his fingers for hours. Someone finally went up to him and said, "For some time now, we've been watching you standing on the corner snapping your fingers. We're curious. What are you trying to do?"

"Oh," the man replied, "If you can keep it a secret, I'll tell you. I'm terrified of elephants, and I'm doing my best to keep them away from me."

Hoping to relieve the poor man, his observer replied, "Sir, don't you know there isn't an elephant within two thousand miles of this place?"

"Yeah," the finger-snapper said gleefully, "you see how good it works?"

Some people are convinced worrying works. Others have been brave enough to discover that the chance their worries will materialize is so small it doesn't pay to worry. Paul shares this bit of practical wisdom with his readers:

"Be careful [anxious, full of care], for nothing; but in everything by prayer and supplication with thanksgiving let your requests be made known unto God. And the peace of God, which passeth all understanding, shall keep your hearts and minds through Christ Jesus."

(Philippians 4:6,7, KJV)

Consider the statistical perspective.

Putting some statistical perspective on our fears helps to weaken their grip on us. However, relying on statistical perspective can also be carried too far.

I'm reminded of the story of a man so fearful of getting on an airplane with a bomb on it that he wouldn't fly. Upon learning that the only way he could include an important convention in his schedule was to fly there, he was terrified. He called his friend Harry, an insurance actuary.

"Hey, Harry, this is George. Do you remember how much I hate to fly? Well, I have to go to a convention next week and the only way I can get there on time is to fly. I'm terrified of getting on a plane with a bomb on it!"

"Oh, George," Harry said, "people don't put bombs on airplanes."

"Nevertheless, Harry, what are my odds?" George persisted.

Harry left the phone to consult his actuarial tables. When he returned, he confidently announced, "Relax, George. There's only one chance in a million you will get on a plane with a bomb on it."

"I knew it," George replied. "It'll happen to me just as sure as I get on that plane. Isn't there anything I can do to improve my odds?"

"Well, wait a minute," Harry said. "Let me check one more thing."

After he had consulted his tables again, Harry announced George's second option. "Yeah, George, there is something else you can do to improve your odds. Take your own bomb on board with you. The chance of getting on a plane with *two* bombs on it is just one in *ten million*."

Try as we will, none of us can take all of the risk out of living. Living *is* risk-taking. But learning not to exaggerate your risks can lower your anxiety level.

Do you fear other people won't like you?

The use of statistical perspective is also an effective way of managing our fear that other people won't like us. As with other unhealthy fears, this one also has to be faced to be conquered. If this is a source of anxiety for you, you might begin to manage it by asking yourself, "What are the chances that everyone I meet will like me?" An honest response to that question requires each of us to admit, "Zero."

Then proceed to ask yourself, "Why should everyone like me? Isn't that expecting too much of people? After all, not everyone who met Jesus liked Him. In fact, even among the twelve He chose to be closest to Him there were two He couldn't count on—one denied Him and the other betrayed Him." You see, even Jesus could only depend on about 85 percent of His friends.

It would be nice if everyone loved you, but is it really necessary? If seven or eight of every ten people you meet like you, isn't that great? With odds like that in your favor when you meet new people, why not assume they *will* like you? And *be surprised when they don't*. This mental posture will help you feel much more comfortable around people *and* increase the chances that they will find you likable.

3. Learn to meditate on Bible scenes.

When you are anxious or afraid, meditate on favorite Bible scenes. The Word of God is filled with passages depicting restful, relaxing scenes upon which you can meditate. Calm can often be restored to an anxious person through the effective use of this kind of mental imagery.

There are those who would deprive the Christian of meditation because New Age thinkers stress its value. However, meditation has always been an important form of Biblical prayer. In Psalm 1:2 (KJV), David says of the "blessed man":

"His delight is in the law of the LORD, and in his law doth he meditate day and night."

This skill helped save the life of a client I'll call Gail.

Teaching Gail to meditate on the Lord and in the Word brought a major breakthrough in her battle for sanity. She was an attractive woman in her late 40s, highly intelligent, and a devoted Christian. Yet, she could not drive herself to her sessions when she first began seeing me for counseling. From the moment she left her house, she was frightened. She was terrified by the bustling traffic on our expressways. So Gail had to depend on her husband or a friend to drive her to her appointments.

In getting acquainted with Gail, I discovered she was very imaginative. Most people who are anxious and fearful have active imaginations, but they are focused on the wrong kind of mental images. Wanting her to discover how her imagination could work *for* her rather than *against* her, I asked, "Gail, what are your three favorite Bible scenes?"

She listed them without hesitation: "The Twenty-third Psalm, The Good Shepherd and the one lost sheep, and Jesus calming the storm on Lake Galilee."

"Good," I said. "Now, I want these scenes to minister to you. First, I want you to take three deep breaths." I gave her the same instructions I gave earlier in this chapter. When she had finished her deep-breathing exercises, dropped her shoulders, and closed her eyes, I suggested, "While your eyes are closed and you are enjoying such a good, relaxed feeling, why don't you picture in your mind the one Bible scene you like most. When you have it in focus, tell me which one it is and describe it for me."

Gail's first choice was the Twenty-third Psalm. She worked with that scene until she could picture the green pastures, locate the stream, see the surrounding hills, hear the sounds of the shepherd's staff against the rocks, and hear the bleating of the sheep. With very little effort, once she got the idea, she was able to fix other favorite Bible scenes in her imagination.

Gail was instructed to take a few moments before leaving the house the next time to recreate one of those scenes in her mind. I reminded her that each of them emphasized the reality of Christ's presence with her everywhere she went. By beginning to focus on an awareness of God's presence and assuring herself that she could do all things through Christ (Philippians 4;13), Gail was able to drive to her sessions after the first five weeks of treatment. She was also able to shop more comfortably.

Every person has some imaginative ability. You can create in your mind scenes you have seen on television or in the movies. Memories of faces and voices from your past are accessible to you. With very little effort, you can no doubt recall pleasant memories of times with family and friends. Using this ability can provide you a very practical tool for reducing anxiety.

4.   Focus on reassuring passages of Scripture.

Practice recalling and meditating on reassuring passages of Scripture. Here are some examples:

"Peace I leave with you, my peace I give unto you: not as the world giveth, give I unto you. Let not your heart be troubled, neither let it be afraid" (John 14:27, KJV).

"Fear thou not; for I am with thee. Be not dismayed; for I am thy God: I will strengthen thee; yea, I will help thee; yea, I will uphold thee with the right hand of my righteousness" (Isaiah 41:10, KJV).

"Ye are of God, little children, and have overcome them: because greater is he that is in you, than he that is in the world" (1 John 4:4, KJV).

"I can do all things through Christ which strengtheneth me" (Philippians 4:13, KJV).

"And we know that all things work together for good to them that love God, to them who are the called according to his purpose" (Romans 8:28, KJV).

"What shall we then say to these things? If God be for us, who can be against us?" (Romans 8:31, KJV).

77

Don't panic!

It is *never* God's will for us to be terrorized by our circumstances. How do I know that? The Word of God tells me. In Matthew 28:20 (KJV), Jesus says, *"Lo, I am with you always, even unto the end of the world."*

Before the angel of the Lord announced Christ's birth to the shepherds, he said, "Fear not." Why did He say that? After all, he had come specifically to give them a wonderful message: detailed information about where they could find baby Jesus.

However, can you imagine how *you* might feel if you had been among those shepherds that night? Their rather routine work of caring for sheep was interrupted by an angelic visitor speaking to them from the night sky. Seeing angelic beings in the middle of the night is enough to frighten anyone.

Had the angel of the Lord *not* helped them manage their fear, they never would have remembered where to find the Christ child. Fear fogs your memory—tends to make you forget. At critical times in our lives when we are overwhelmed with fear and anxiety, it is easy for us to miss creative options God wants to provide for us.

Many of the people I see in counseling miss tremendous opportunities in life because of their anxiety over feeling self-conscious. No one is born self-conscious. This is something people acquire over a period of time after they are here. It is the feeling of being observed—but not approved. A Biblical approach to dealing with this common form of anxiety can help you manage it better.

Remember, God does not make you feel self-conscious.

Self-consciousness can be so uncomfortable and preoccupying that it can mentally paralyze you. For example, regardless of how experienced a speaker may be, if an audience begins to act disinterested or look at him in a disapproving way, it becomes increasingly difficult for him to think clearly and to express himself well. Self-consciousness can be that crippling.

Paul did not want Timothy to be intimidated by enemies of the gospel. He did not want to see Timothy's ministry hindered by self-consciousness. That's one of the first things Paul draws to Timothy's attention in his second letter to the young man.

In the first chapter, Paul identifies Phygellus and Hermogenes as being among Timothy's contemporaries in Asia who had turned away from Paul's ministry of the gospel. He wants to be sure Timothy doesn't come under the influence of this group (2 Timothy 1:13-15).

He reminds Timothy that his faith is the product of three generations of his family. He challenges Timothy to greater enthusiasm in his ministry and assures him of God's help in giving a clear, unmistakable testimony of the gospel.

"When I call to remembrance the unfeigned faith that is in thee, which dwelt first in thy grandmother Lois, and thy mother Eunice; and I am persuaded that in thee also, Wherefore I put thee in remembrance that thou stir up the gift of God, which is in thee by the putting on of my hands. For God hath not given us the spirit of fear; but of power, and of love, and of a sound mind" (2 Timothy 1:5-7, KJV).

The Greek word translated "fear" can be more accurately understood to mean "self-consciousness." Paul's reference to a "sound mind" is not a reflection of his concern for Timothy's mental health. Rather, he is assuring Timothy that God has equipped us with power and love which enable us to overcome the anxiety of self-consciousness so that we can think clearly, express ourselves clearly, and be effective in bearing testimony to Christ before the world.

If you are self-conscious, take 2 Timothy 1:7 as God's Word to you. God has not made you self-conscious. The roots of your self-consciousness are probably so deep in your past that you have no memory of a time in your life when you were *not* self-conscious.

Home environments which produce self-conscious children are created by parents who are difficult to please and frequently believe that children are to be seen and not heard. This is the kind of parent who responds to a report card of four "A" grades and one "B" grade with, "Why the B?" Children raised in this kind of home often feel they are being observed, but very seldom feel approved.

Your heavenly Father is not hard to please!

Paul assures Timothy that our heavenly Father is not like many earthly parents. He is observing us all the time, *and most of the time He is approving of us in Jesus.*

This is a new kind of Christianity for many people. It has never dawned on them that God is pleased with their lives most of the time. In fact, many Christians are happy to get through a day when they feel like their heavenly Father is *not displeased* with them. For the most part, their goal is to avoid God's wrath.

Yet, the Bible makes it clear that God is not reluctant to brag on His children. In Job 2:3 (KJV), God says as much to Satan:

"Hast thou considered my servant Job, that there is none like him in the earth, a perfect and an upright man, one that feareth God, and escheweth evil?"

Jesus' yoke is easy—His burden is light.

Nothing will revolutionize your relationship with God more than understanding how easy it is to gain your heavenly Father's approval. After all, *Jesus did not say,* "Come unto me, all ye that

80

labor and are heavy laden—and I will give you a nervous breakdown." He said:

> *"Come unto me, all ye that labor and are heavy laden, and I will give you rest. Take my yoke upon you, and learn of me; for I am meek and lowly in heart: and ye shall find rest unto your souls. For my yoke is easy, and my burden is light"* (Matthew 11:28-30, KJV).

God wants us to know that He is not only *observing* us all the time but *most of the time He is approving of us, in Jesus.* What does that do to your self-consciousness?

God gives His children power.

Paul told Timothy that God has given us power, not fear and self-consciousness. What kind of power has God given us? First of all, God has given us the power to be called His children.

> *"But as many as received him, to them gave he power to become the sons of God, even to them that believe on his name"* (John 1:12, KJV).

The Greek word John uses for power is "exousia," which literally means "authority." God has given me the authority to become His child. No one becomes a child of God by human choice alone, however; each one who enters God's family takes his place there through an expression of God's will.

The second kind of power God gives the Christian is defined by the Greek word "zoe," for which the English translation is "everlasting life" or "eternal life."

> *"For God so loved the world, that he gave his only begotten Son, that whosoever believeth in him should not perish, but have everlasting life"* (John 3:16, KJV).

This is the same power by which Christ, as the Word, made all things out of nothing:

81

"All things were made by him; and without him was not anything made that was made. In him was life...."

(John 1:3,4, KJV)

What creative power! In Chapter 7 of this book, I will have more to say about its application in the affairs of our daily lives.

The third kind of power God gives us is the kind Christ refers to in Acts 1:8 (KJV):

"But ye shall receive power, after that the Holy Ghost is come upon you: and ye shall be witnesses unto me both in Jerusalem, and in all Judea, and in Samaria, and unto the uttermost part of the earth."

Here the Greek word is "dunamis," from which we derive our English words "dynamo" and "dynamite." Both of these words are energy-related. A dynamo provides a continual flow of energy. Dynamite is expressed in a sudden burst of energy. In giving this power to believers, Jesus provides the energy required for their expression of an effective witness to His gospel. Sometimes this power may be expressed very boldly as in miracles, signs, and healing. Usually it takes the form of a light continuing to shine in the darkness.

The purpose of these gifts of power is to provide us with the courage to reach beyond our fears and anxieties to love:

"For God hath not given us the spirit of fear; but of power, and of love..." (2 Timothy 1:7, KJV).

As we experience this confidence and love, we grow out of our anxiety into the courage to overcome our self-consciousness. Then we are able to reach out and confidently share God's love with those around us.

God watches you with loving eyes.

When Isaac Watts was a boy, he lived next door to an elderly Christian lady who took a special interest in him. He sensed her love for him, so he visited her often. One day she noticed how fascinated Isaac was with a Scripture motto on her wall. The passage came from Genesis 16:13. It was Hagar's prayer in the desert after she was cast out of Abraham's home. This brief motto simply said, *"Thou God seest me."*

Because of his interest in it, the old lady decided to give Isaac the motto. As she took it down from the wall and handed it to him, she said, "Son, I want you to have this. When you get older, you'll meet people who will want to make you believe that this Scripture means God is following you with a judgmental eye, watching you everywhere you go; seeing everything you do; searching for some reason to judge you. Don't you believe them. *What this passage really means is that God loves you so much He just can't take His eyes off of you."*

Your natural parents may have left you feeling like they were always observing you—but seldom approving you. You may have brought into your adult life *very crippling* dimensions of self-consciousness from your past. However, as a Christian, you need to know that your heavenly Father does not view you that way. He is always observing you *because He loves you so much He just can't take His eyes off of you.* And—most of the time—*He is approving of you!*

In determining to defeat unhealthy fear in your life, you may want to make a list of sources of fear and anxiety. Be sure to review the four methods of conquering fear we have discussed and then determine which you believe will be most effective for you. Once again, they are:

1. Practice deep-breathing exercises.

2. Apply a statistical perspective to fears and anxieties.

3. Create restful, meditative Bible images in your mind.

4. Learn to focus on reassuring passages of Scripture.

As you begin to apply these suggestions to the fears you must face in your life, the Lord may help you to defeat some of them almost instantly. However, it is more likely that you will overcome most of them gradually. This is the way it happened for David. Early in his life, David said, *"What time I am afraid, I will trust in thee"* (Psalm 56:3, KJV). When he was older and had learned to overcome his fears, he wrote, *"The LORD is on my side; I will not fear: what can man do unto me?"* (Psalm 118:6, KJV). David had learned to conquer his fears and anxieties in God's strength. So can you.

Learning to come to terms with fear and anxiety will help you become more confident in your approach to life. This *may* result in your becoming aware of angry feelings you have previously been too anxious to acknowledge.

In our next chapter, I will suggest some practical ways for getting in touch with your angry feelings and putting them to work for you—because anger makes a *good servant,* but a *poor master.*

Chapter 4

Anger: Master or Servant?

What does it take to make you angry?

Many church people have a tendency to see any expression of anger as being at least undesirable, if not downright sinful. In fact, many Christians believe anger is the result of the fall of mankind.

However, when God created Adam and Eve, He gave them the ability to experience anger and express aggression. Before the fall, God gave them this commission:

". . . Replenish the earth, and subdue it; and have dominion over the fish of the sea, and over the fowl of the air, and over every living thing that moveth upon the earth."
(Genesis 1:28, KJV)

Anger and aggression were to equip Adam for his task.

Adam and Eve had a twofold task. They were to *subdue* the earth and *have dominion over it.* Without an anger drive and the ability to be aggressive, Adam and Eve would have been unable

85

to subdue the earth *or* have dominion over it. After all, if one is going to subdue *anything*, one *cannot be passive.*

So, you see, anger and aggression were part of the original emotional equipment God gave Adam and Eve for carrying out their task. Experienced and expressed in healthy ways, these feelings provide the intensity and energy for an effective life.

Anger makes a poor master.

However, as a result of the fall, anger has become one of man's worst enemies. Uncontrolled or misdirected, it can complicate or even destroy one's life. Only God knows how many personal lives, marriages, and families have been wrecked by anger gone awry.

Anger makes a poor master. However, it can be harnessed and turned into a very productive servant. What follows has been written to help you break out of bondage to your anger and learn how to make it your servant.

You can't start too soon!

We begin our battle with anger shortly after we are born. As soon as parental love relieves us of infant fears, each of us becomes secure enough to demonstrate anger. Any mother knows what infant rage is. The first time her soft, tender little bundle of love stiffens, reddens, and screams, she knows he has begun his lifelong bout with anger.

The limits parents begin to set on their infant's behavior inevitably frustrate him. If he has been loved enough to feel secure, he will vent his frustration in an angry test of those limits. For the child, learning to manage angry moments in ways that meet with his parents' approval is an essential lesson in survival.

In many homes, when little people get angry it results in big people getting angry. And when big people in the home get angry little people can no longer afford the luxury of expressing their anger or any *other* negative feelings. A child raised in this kind of home quickly learns to hide his feelings as much as possible.

**Few children are taught how to
manage their angry moments.**

Although children learn how parents do *not* want them to express their anger, few parents are thoughtful enough to teach their children approved ways of *expressing* it. As a result, children often learn to feel guilty for experiencing anger and downright sinful for expressing it.

The national scope of this problem was evident two decades ago. In their 1974 report, the Joint Commission on the Mental Health of Children said:

"The role of violence and its encouragement in young children must be faced squarely. Some children meet abuse and angry outbursts at the hand of their parents. Nearly all children are exposed to graphic violence over the television screen. Through possible imitation of and identification with these models, patterns of violent behavior may be easily acquired.

"Of at least equal importance are the patterns by which the young child is taught to handle his own frustrations, his own angry feelings, and the constructive or destructive acts for which he comes to feel responsible. Possibly no other area represents as profound a source of pathology in our culture as the handling of anger and aggression."

Hopefully, children raised in Christian families are subject to less violence in their families and in the kinds of entertainment they see. However, they probably receive no more training in how to deal positively with anger than their peers in secular families. If this statement startles you, then remember that being angry—to some Christians—means being "bad." With many, anger is not only a misdemeanor . . . it's a felony. When parents view anger this way, their response to it is likely to be punitive and suppressive rather than instructive. However, the Bible does not treat anger that way. In Psalm 7:11 (KJV), David reveals that, *"God is angry with the wicked every day."*

Jesus knew what it was to be angry.

Believe it or not, the third chapter of the Gospel of Mark records the fact that *even Jesus experienced anger—and He expressed it!*

The Pharisees wanted to find some reason to condemn Jesus. Finding Him in the synagogue on the Sabbath, they tried to trick Him into breaking the Sabbath.

A man was there with a withered hand. The Pharisees watched to see if Jesus would violate the Sabbath by healing him. It was obvious to the Lord that the Pharisees were more interested in Him keeping the Sabbath than they were in helping this poor, crippled man. Jesus was angered by this and decided to heal the man on the spot. Mark puts it this way:

"And he entered again into the synagogue; and there was a man there which had a withered hand. And they watched him, whether he would heal him on the sabbath day; that they might accuse him. And he saith unto the man which had the withered hand, Stand forth. And he said unto them, is it lawful to do good on the Sabbath days, or to do evil? to save life, or to kill? But they held their peace. And when he had looked 'round about on them with anger, being grieved for the hardness of their hearts, he saith unto the man, Stretch forth thine hand. And he stretched it out; and his hand was restored whole as the other. And the Pharisees went forth and straightway took counsel with the Herodians against him, how they might destroy him."

(Mark 3:1-6, KJV)

88

Anger is a normal human emotion.

If God is angry with the wicked every day, and even Jesus experienced anger, then maybe our fear of our own anger and subsequent guilt are *exaggerated reactions to a normal human emotion.* To help you deal with your fear of anger, I want to share with you a simple four-step formula for managing it. Putting this formula into practice in your life will help you live more comfortably with your own anger.

1.   **Accept anger as a fact of your life.**

Like the common cold, anger is a recurrent life experience. You may not like it, but you can't ignore it and stay healthy. Resolutions about never becoming angry again only add more fuel to the fire the next time you are angry—so forget them!

Anger is the second emotion we learn to experience; only fear precedes it. As mentioned earlier, anger is first expressed as infant rage.

At that point, no guilt is associated with it. You have to *learn* to feel guilty for being angry. However, most of us were taught to feel guilty about our anger so early in our infancy that we cannot remember a time when we didn't.

Of course, when expressions of anger are undisciplined and destructive, it is healthy to feel guilty. However, the energy produced by anger does not have to be expressed in undisciplined ways.

All of us should be concerned about the dangerous side effects undisciplined anger may have. This is the issue Paul addressed in writing to the Ephesian church: *"Be ye angry, and sin not: let not the sun go down upon your wrath"* (Ephesians 4:26, KJV).

Unfortunately, instead of seeing this as a command from Paul to learn healthy ways of managing anger, many believers have seen it as implying that if you are a "good" Christian, you never get angry. They take a very legalistic view of this passage, implying from it that if you get mad you're a "bad" Christian. And if you stay mad overnight, you're "really bad!"

Actually, Paul is saying that as long as we are human, we will have to come to terms with anger. He is urging us to learn how to manage it promptly, effectively, and constructively. Once we can do that, we no longer need to be afraid of our anger. Then, with the Lord's help, we can put each day's conflicts to rest with the sunset.

"Yes, you are!" "No, I'm not!" "Yes, you are!"

Christians who see anger as inconsistent with their faith must either deny their anger or confess it as sin. Unfortunately, it is much easier to deny it. So, Christians who are uncomfortable admitting they get angry must find some other word to describe the same feeling. They can admit to being terribly upset, nervous, frustrated, irritated, disappointed, or even furious much more easily than they can admit to being angry.

Can you imagine how ridiculous it must be to observe two such believers engage in a heated argument? As the conflict increases, voices are raised, the muscles stand out in one brother's neck, and a sharp edge comes into his voice. His face reddens— and then his more "spiritual" brother says, condemningly, "Why, brother, you're angry."

And the other brother responds in a strained voice, "I am not angry."

Of course, any neutral observer of such a confrontation would realize that both men were extremely angry at the moment. However, admitting it would leave them both feeling that they weren't very good Christians because of their mutual deeply rooted conviction that "good Christians don't get angry."

90

The apostles creatively managed anger.

Can you imagine the apostles arguing and debating the differences between the Jews and Gentiles in the church at the Council of Jerusalem without raising their voices? In recording that historic event, Luke honestly acknowledges their agreement only came about after "... *much disputing*"(Acts 15:7).

The participants in this heated argument were not only "good Christians," they were apostles and elders of the church (Acts 15:6). There is no hint that this heated exchange of sharp differences was a negative reflection on their spirituality. In fact, this is a Biblical illustration of the creative management of conflict.

It is healthier to view anger as a normal human emotion that everyone must learn to accept and deal with in daily life than to pretend that it doesn't exist in the life of a healthy believer. *The fact that you experience anger in no way implies that you should consider yourself less spiritual than others.*

Perhaps it will be easier for you to develop this attitude if you begin to see anger for what it really is. In its simplest form—

Anger is unexpressed energy.

Physiologically, this is exactly what it is. When your mind interprets a situation as threatening, a biochemical reaction is triggered. This results in the creation of unusually large amounts of energy for you to use in facing the perceived threat. Your emotion—anger—is thus transformed into physical energy.

Think for a moment of what that means. Do you remember your high school physics class? Einstein discovered that under certain conditions *matter can be destroyed*—but insisted that *energy cannot be destroyed;* it can only be transformed.

Once you are angry, you are in possession of energy which cannot be destroyed. Until you determine what form the expression of your energy will take, you have committed no sin. Your moral challenge is this: *You are responsible to determine what you will do with the energy your anger has created.*

If a person can't admit he is angry, he will have great difficulty learning healthy ways of discharging the energy his anger has created. Therefore, the first step in our formula for anger management is simply to accept anger as a fact of your life. Realize that you are entitled to experience anger without guilt or shame so long as you learn to express it appropriately.

Anger appears at unexpected times.

When you are able to accept your anger, you may find it showing up at unexpected times. Often when people are grieving, they are aware of anger. They may feel so embarrassed and guilty about this that they can't discuss it even with their closest friend. Yet, this is such a common experience that few people suffer the loss of loved ones without going through it. Their anger may not make sense, but it is real. Sometimes they are angry at their loved one for dying and leaving them. They may be angry at the medical team for not being able to save their loved one. At times, they are angry with God for permitting the events to happen.

How do you help someone in these circumstances? Let them know these feelings are common among people going through similar experiences. Encourage them to express their anger to God. You'll discover this is very difficult for them to do.

People fear that if they express anger to God, He may in turn get angry at them. They have vivid mental pictures of how angry their parents became with them when they became angry as children. They must be reminded that their heavenly Father is not like an earthly parent who may respond to a child's anger by becoming furious with the child.

2. Become aware of your anger.

Unrecognized anger is far more dangerous to us than that which we are able to accept and recognize. When you learn to accept your anger, no one has to tell you you're angry. You are aware of it. You know you're angry.

When you know that you are angry, you can choose from among several healthy and appropriate ways of expressing it. However, if you insist on denying your anger, you are likely to express it in ways that damage your relationships with the important people in your life.

Big boys don't cry.

Our culture brutalizes its males. Little boys are taught to grow callouses on their feelings. Because of this, we men are at a real disadvantage when it comes to recognizing our emotions.

For example, when little sister falls down and skins her knee, she comes crying to mother or dad for comfort. She is taken up in their arms, given some affection, and assured that everything will be all right. When brother falls down, he comes running to a parent expecting the same treatment. After all, his knee hurts just as much. But as often as not, the parent may take him by the shoulder, jerk him a little bit, and say, "Oh, hush! Don't you know big boys don't cry?"

In informal ways like this, boys learn that a man in our culture is not expected to show his emotions. We expect our men to be "tough." Unfortunately, part of being tough or strong means that males must learn to be insensitive to feelings. This is a part of the male's traditional preparation for bearing the brunt of the military obligation and job market competition in our highly materialistic society.

Little girls are allowed to feel comfortable with being emotional, but they still grow into women who most likely deny being angry. Little boys are taught to hide their feelings. As a result, they often hide *from* their feelings.

This difference in the way males and females are socialized is widely recognized among Americans. In fact, it is built into our sense of humor. Men jokingly remark that the woman's motto is, "If at first you don't succeed, cry, cry again!"

Take a personal safari!

If you are going to become aware of anger in your life, you are going to have to go on a search for it and be determined to find it. Begin to look for the places in your life where you think you may be unconsciously hiding anger.

Look underneath words you may be using to disguise your anger. Catch yourself saying things like: *I'm fed up. I've had it. I'm sick and tired of that. That burns me up. I can't swallow that. He makes me sick. She makes me sick to my stomach. I'm disgusted. You make me laugh.*

Here's one that really hides the anger: *I'm hurt.* At EMERGE, we won't permit our clients to say they are *hurt* unless they are willing to acknowledge at the same time that they are *angry.* After all, how can someone hurt you without making you angry? People resist acknowledging this. They will say, "I'm just so hurt."

And I will insist, "And angry."

"Oh, no!" they object. "I'm not angry—I'm just hurt."

Then I explain, "If someone came in here and hit me in the face, I can predict two simultaneous feelings would surface in me. One would be pain. The other would be anger. Yes, I would be hurt—but I would also be angry. Don't just recognize one of those feelings—acknowledge them both!"

Usually the person will say, "Well, when you put it like that, I see what you're talking about. I guess *I am angry and hurt.*"

94

Don't hide your anger from yourself.

Unfortunately, the church has allowed believers to identify with the pain of a hurtful experience but not with the anger. It's okay for believers to say, "I'm hurt," but it's not okay for them to say "I'm angry."

As a result of this kind of religious training, it is extremely difficult for Christians to say they are angry when their children are living contrary to the way they have been raised. Instead, they say, "My children are breaking my heart."

Who are we kidding? Of course, once in a while our children behave in ways that hurt us. But I can tell you without any hesitation that when my children hurt me they also tick me off. When they behave in ways that make me look like a failure as a parent, I'm not only hurt—I'm angry.

When I go to church I'm smart enough not to tell folks there that I'm angry with my child. I make sure I tell the people at church that I'm "burdened" for my children. Or, if I want to appear even more spiritual, I will say, "My child is breaking my heart."

Of course, there's nothing wrong with simply sharing the pain of your parental experiences with your friends at church. However, you should know yourself well enough to know that mixed in with the pain and sadness of what you are experiencing is some anger. Even if you feel it is socially desirable to hide your anger from others, don't hide it from yourself. You can deal with it much more effectively once you get it out in the open. Become aware of your anger!

Look for anger in episodes of depression.

Depression is another hiding place for anger. More frequently than not, situational depression is aggravated if not initially caused by anger which the person unconsciously turns inward as a form of temporary self-hatred. However, depressed people seldom recognize themselves as being angry. They say things like, *I feel blue. I'm really down. I wish I were dead. Sometimes I just feel like killing myself.*

It never ceases to amaze me that people can be suicidal and still deny that they are angry. In an effort to put these desperate people in touch with their anger, I have often said to them, "It must be very painful to be so angry with yourself."

Almost invariably, they reply in genuine amazement, "What makes you think I am angry with myself?"

Often they are unable to become aware of their anger unless someone directly points it out to them. Sometimes I have been successful in helping such a person see his hidden anger by saying something like, "Well, I've always believed that before you could bring yourself to kill someone, you had to be very angry with that person—even if it happens to be yourself." It is interesting to see some of these people as they get in touch with their anger toward themselves for the first time.

In most of the depressed people I have seen, there is a large amount of disguised anger. Once the person recognizes it and begins to become aware of it, they have taken an important step toward recovery. We'll pursue a more complete discussion of anger's role in depression in a later chapter.

Living with a depressed person can be anger-provoking.

Years ago, when my first wife was battling post-partum depression following the birth of our first child, I didn't understand what she was going through. All I knew was that I would come home day after day and find her depressed. At that time, I hadn't learned how to come to terms with someone else's feelings. I didn't know how to give her the emotional support she needed from me. This was frustrating for her.

When I would come home and find her still depressed, I would say really brilliant things—like, "Oh, no, not again!" Worse yet, "Honey, you know, I don't know what to do. I try and try to be the best husband I can and it doesn't seem to help."

Both of these statements are full of anger. I wonder how I was so blind as to not see it. In the first instance, I was unconsciously trying to get my wife to hide her depression from me. It produced a feeling of powerlessness in me that was too painful for me to tolerate. In the second instance, I was hoping my wife would feel so guilty for presenting me with such a depressed mate that she would just "snap out of it."

"They shall be comforted."

Then, one day, when I found her on the verge of tears, the Holy Spirit prompted me to put my arms around her, tuck her head on my shoulder, and say to her, "Honey, go ahead and let your feelings out. You'll feel better when you've cried and gotten your feelings out of you."

Immediately she began to sob her heart out. I hadn't said anything magical, but when she was finished crying she had gotten some of her feelings out of her. She not only felt better, but I had grown considerably taller in her estimation because I had learned to communicate with her at the level of her feelings.

Since that time, I have become increasingly aware of how deceptive a person's mind can be in attempting to avoid angry feelings. If you want to become aware of your anger, you must learn to look for it in places where you think it may be hiding.

Look for your anger in your nonverbal behavior.

Are you an angry driver? How fierce are you in competitive sports? How do you react when your side loses in party games? How much do you grind your teeth? How do you react when someone keeps you waiting?

Get curious about where your anger may be hiding from you. You are much more likely to manage anger maturely if you

97

learn to recognize it early in its rise so you can control your anger *before it overwhelms you.*

"Oh, my aching back!"

Because anger affects you physiologically, learn to identify its presence in your body. Get curious about what happens to you physically as you begin to get angry. Where in your body do you first become conscious of anger? I can feel my neck muscles tighten. My shoulders get tense. A sharp edge can be heard in my voice. People literally give me a pain in the neck.

Where do you experience anger? Some people first become aware of it in the cardiovascular area. Others develop lower back pain. Some experience anger in the gastrointestinal tract. Others have difficulty breathing. What happens in your body? Where do you feel anger?

Why is this important? The earlier you detect anger, the sooner you can impose your spiritual controls for it. This brings us to the third step in our formula for anger management . . .

3. Control your anger.

Our maturity is measured by our ability to accept our emotions, become aware of them, and control them. The most mature person is the one who is most in touch with his feelings and who has best control of them.

A person's spiritual maturity can be measured by the size of the things that make them angry. The more spiritually mature person is in control of his anger.

By accepting and detecting anger, a person can gain the advance notice he needs to impose his controls. This prevents the embarrassment that would result from an undisciplined display of anger.

Marriage tests your control of anger.

Your needs for control will be put to the test in marriage. In this most intimate of relationships you not only have your own angry feelings to contend with at times, but you also have to learn how to deal with your partner's anger.

When you see your mate out of control, the wisest and most loving thing you can do is retreat. Give your mate a chance to regain composure. When things have settled down, if you have been that considerate, your mate will probably apologize. More important—your mate will have seen an example of the benefit that comes from gaining spiritual control over anger.

Parents get angry.

Parenthood pushes most of us beyond our limits of control at times. Perhaps the best way to manage those times is to apologize to the child. Children are among the world's most forgiving people. The humiliation of having to ask your child to forgive you for letting your anger get the best of you should help you have better control in future dealings with the child.

If you've already heard the following story, you'll agree that it helps illustrate the previous point.

A mother heard her four-year-old son screaming and crying from the basement where he was watching his father build cupboards. Fearing the boy had been seriously hurt, she opened the basement door and saw him sobbing there at the bottom of the steps.

"What in the world is wrong with you?" she asked.

Through his tears, the little guy volunteered, "Daddy hit his thumb with the hammer."

"If daddy hit his thumb with the hammer, then why are you crying?" she asked.

"Well ... I didn't cry at first," he said between sobs. "I laughed."

Your honesty in apologizing to your child after an episode like this also establishes a good base for requiring your child to apologize to other family members when he has lost his temper. The pain of having to ask others' forgiveness is a tool the *child's* conscience can also use to provide better control of anger in the future.

There's a place for healthy anger. Just stay in control. Remember Jesus' mood when He chased the money changers out of the temple. Remaining calm and unruffled when your children have seriously misbehaved would be failing them as a parent. However, try to remember the difference between "motes" and "beams." Don't pull out the cannon to go hunting for gnats. This kind of approach to young people frequently wins the battle, but loses the war.

Because teenagers can argue so eloquently in their own defense, some parents get drawn into shouting matches with them. Often only a minor point divides the two of them—but once their tempers are ignited, a major battle is waged. Such a situation reminds me of a preacher who reviewed his Sunday sermon outline and discovered that one point was very weak. Rather than strengthen or eliminate that point, he chose to note in the margin, "Point weak. Shout here."

When a parent has to get into a shouting match with a teenager, it indicates to the young person that the parent's case is weak. If your case is strong enough, you don't need to shout to make it stick.

Learn how to keep your "cool" as a parent.

Remember the three Fs of good discipline. Be **fair**. How do you go about being fair? You try to put yourself in the child's place—no matter what his age—and ask yourself, "If I were in this circumstance and four years old; nine years old; sixteen years old; what could I reasonably be expected to be responsible for doing or saying?" Try to put yourself in your child's place to determine what is fair to expect. If the limits you have set for your youngster are fair, you don't have to shout to defend them. If the responsibilities you outline for your children are fair, you don't have to apologize for them. If they aren't, then no amount of loud talk will make them fair. Change them. Make them fair. Once you know you are being fair as a parent, you can afford to be **firm**. Many parents cannot be firm unless they are angry. However, you don't have to be angry to be firm. The fact that you know you are being *fair* should help you be *firm* without being angry.

Be friendly. Teenagers are more likely to respect firmness that is friendly than firmness that is angry. Remember, they are masters of passive aggression. They know how to keep their cool while they are needling you into losing yours.

"I'm only doing what you told me to do."

If you want to feel what it is like to have someone's passive aggression aimed at you, try to put yourself in one father's place. The family had been seated at the table several minutes, waiting for the oldest son to take his place. At last he rushed into the dining room, sat down at the table, and bowed his head. His father noticed that the boy's hands were filthy.

He said to his son, "You know bettter than to come to the table with hands like that. Go upstairs and wash your hands." The family waited patiently for him. Finally, after several more minutes, his father impatiently shouted, "What's taking you so long? Get back down here!"

The son replied with a whine in his voice, "I'm only doing what you told me to do."

For a parent *not to feel provoked* by that kind of behavior is asking too much. However, I would hope that a wise parent would learn not to fall into the trap, lose his cool, and consequently lash out at the boy.

It takes practice to refuse the bait. But the first time you succeed, you will feel wonderful. Get wise to the tactics of your teenagers. Be sure your case is strong and fair. Once you know you are fair, then be firm—and stay friendly.

God wants the energy created by your anger to be expressed constructively. If turning your anger into constructive action is a problem for you, let me give you some simple rules to help you get on top of your anger.

In His Sermon on the Mount, Jesus makes it clear that the less control a person has over his anger, the more serious the consequences he must face:

> *"But I say unto you, That whosoever is angry with his brother without a cause shall be in danger of the judgment: and whosoever shall say to his brother, Raca, shall be in danger of the council: but whosoever shall say, Thou fool, shall be in danger of hell fire"* (Matthew 5:22, KJV).

Notice that if you are *angry without a cause* you are only in danger of *judgment.* So far, you have said nothing. Once impulse control is lost and the friend is called an *idiot (Raca)*, you are in danger of *the council.* If you throw constraint to the winds and *curse your brother (calling him a fool),* then you are in danger of *hell fire.*

The principle Jesus is teaching here is clear. The less control a person has over his anger, the more serious are the consequences he must face. This not only defines the way God deals with us, but it also usually defines the way anger management works in daily life.

Avoid clamming up!

First of all, in your efforts to control anger, let me suggest that you avoid "clamming up." People who attempt to control anger by clamming up risk damaging their physical health.

Psychosomatic illnesses feed on unexpressed anger. God has not designed your body to accommodate large amounts of unexpressed anger over long periods of time.

As much as possible, the energy created by the anger, conflict, tension, and pressure of the day needs to be released before the day's end. If you don't develop ways of getting that energy out of you through creative or nondestructive activities, sooner or later it will find symptomatic expression among your weakest organic systems. So, consciously work at transforming the energy created by anger into useful activities that either will help you get your day's agenda done or keep you physically fit. Don't "clam up" and run the risk of damaging your physical health.

Avoid blowing up!

The second extreme method of managing anger you will want to avoid is "blowing up." When you blow up, you damage your relationships. If you don't say it, there will be nothing for you to try to forget. If you don't do it, there will be nothing for you to have to remember.

There are better ways of managing your anger than to resort to either of these extremes. If you are in control of anger, you don't suffer the long-term consequences of its control over you. When your anger gets control of you, you say and do things that complicate your life. Often, you create circumstances that are difficult, if not impossible, to reverse. Anger out of control can destroy your family. Therefore, conscious awareness of anger becomes important in alerting you to your needs for control.

Suggestions for controlling your anger . . .

First, learn to identify the source of your anger. Are you simply angry at life, or is there someone in particular who has angered you? Are you angry at specific situations or circumstances in your life? Who or what has angered you?

103

Second, determine if the degree of your anger is appropriate. If someone else were in the same situation, is it likely they would feel the same way?

Third, apply your controls! Build up a repertoire of control behaviors which seem to work reasonably well for you. Let me make some suggestions. Suppose you and your mate are in a verbal battle. You have reached that familiar point in your argument where you're both generating more heat than light. There doesn't seem to be any solution and you can feel yourself losing control. At that point, why not just say to your mate "Honey, I need some time out. Give me a few minutes to cool off."

Then put some physical space between the two of you. Go to another room. Change your activity. Get busy doing something to take your mind off things temporarily. Doing this with your mate's permission will help you regain your composure.

If your mate has the good sense to give you "time out" when you ask for it, then be fair enough to extend them the same courtesy the next time they need it. When you see they are overloaded with tension, anxiety, and anger, give them some relief. Let them back out of the argument for a few minutes.

Often, something as simple as silently counting from one to ten will give you enough time and emotional distance to overcome your tendency to let them have your "zinger."

If counting to ten doesn't seem to be an adequate way for you to maintain control, then try something that takes a little longer. Try saying The Lord's Prayer silently. Any simple behavior will work if it helps you avoid a hasty response you will regret later. I have met many people who would do anything possible to undo something they said in a moment of impulsive anger.

Another good control mechanism is to go for a walk. Please note, *I am not suggesting you go for a drive.* It is unsafe to drive when you are extremely angry. However, taking a walk is an excellent way to cool off.

If you decide to use this way of regaining control, I hope your mate is not like the woman whose husband was about to attempt it. She yelled at him: "If you walk out of this house now, I'll follow you out on the sidewalk and scream at you until everybody in this neighborhood knows what I have to put up with!"

Assure your mate that your request for "time out" doesn't mean you are trying to avoid the subject of the controversy. If the matter is important enough to produce that much friction between partners, it is too important to postpone indefinitely. However, once both partners have established a track record of good faith by picking up the discussion in better control at a future time, it should be easier to tolerate these delays.

Take time to develop some of these simple controls. With their help, you will experience the good feeling of getting through intense conflict with your self-respect intact and your anger in control.

Count on some storms.

It is too much to expect that most couples can live together without times of conflict. After all, how can a husband and wife know intense pleasure and intimacy without also knowing intense pain and conflict at times? If you are an intense person, you are not only intense in expressing your pleasure, but you are also intense in your anger. And in those moments of intense pain and conflict between mates, it is important to recognize the need for some time and space to regain composure.

When we get away for a few minutes, our emotions calm down. We can put a more rational perspective on what's happening. Then we can come together again, resume the subject, and resolve the difference without an explosion. Unfortunately, most Christians have the impression that if their marriages are what they should be, mates seldom disagree or have heated arguments. Occasionally I see a couple who try to impress me by telling me, "Well, we may have our faults, but one thing our children will have to admit—they have never heard us raise our voices at each other."

It may not be appropriate for me to challenge this statement at the time, but you can be sure I am saying to myself, "If they don't raise their voices at each other, how in the world *do* they manage their anger?" Some quieter ways can be just as damaging to a marriage as intensely loud arguments.

God intends for your anger to be your servant—not your master! Once you have accepted anger as a fact of your life, have become aware of where your body registers it, and acquired some effective methods of control, you are in a position to direct the energy your anger produces into creative or recreational activities.

4.   Direct your anger.

It is simpler to teach young children the skill of redirecting anger's energy than it is to teach adults. If you have children at home, give them *permission to be angry* and *a choice of energy-demanding things to do* when they are angry so that their angry feelings will not necessarily cost them your approval.

When your children choose to do things you have defined for them to do when they're angry, compliment them. Say things to them like, "I know you were very angry this morning, but it was really neat for me to see the way you managed your anger. I was really proud of that. How did you feel about the way you behaved?" Then listen to the feedback. It will help you know what they are thinking as they learn to manage their angry moments. A simple plan like this can help your children grow up having control over their anger most of the time.

106

There's hope for adults, too!

Your parents may not have taught you positive ways of dealing with anger, but your heavenly Father can still help you get control of your anger regardless of your age. Anyone who is willing to work at it can tame anger. God will help you with the process. Here are some steps to follow:

1. Be determined to succeed.

As you read this, you can make up your mind that anger has controlled you long enough. Now, with God's help, you are going to gain control over it. Commitment to succeed is an essential first step in the battle.

2. Sublimate your anger.

In the beginning of your battle with your temper, realize this is a joint effort between you and God. Remember, the energy created by your anger can be used in many different ways.

A regular exercise/workout program will serve the interest of your physical health and help you discharge the energy generated in moments of anger.

If you prefer more recreational activities, your anger can be expressed in jogging, racquetball, golf, or any other sport you find enjoyable. The more skilled you become in accepting and detecting your anger, the more capable you will be of putting its energy to healthy use.

The reformers certainly made a friend of their anger and used its energy in their causes. Martin Luther said, "I can preach better when I'm angry." I don't recommend that for healthy pulpit preaching, but there are ways to harness the energy anger creates to build excitement, motivate people, intensify their interest, and spark their enthusiasm for worthy causes.

Become angry at such social issues as illiteracy, poverty, social prejudice, drunk driving, pornography, and violence in entertainment media—particularly on the television screen, which is so accessible to impressionable children and young teens. Such worthwhile causes offer you another excellent way to creatively use the energy created by your anger.

3. Be patient with yourself.

In getting control over anger in your life, be patient. This is not a single step of growth for most people. It is a journey. However, every journey must begin with a first step. Begin now to apply the simple insights I have shared with you in the management of your anger.

Ask God to help you with this battle. It is often difficult for believers to associate prayer with anything less than total healing. Improvement that comes with effort on their part appears to them to be more from a source of human help than divine. However, victory over anger is not likely to occur all at once. Once you make the commitment, God will help you win this battle for control of your anger. Learn to thank Him for every measure of success you experience along the way.

4. Thank God for any sign of improvement.

Thank God for miracles! Where would we be without them? However, the fact that we call them "miracles" identifies them as exceptional and rare. If this was the typical way believers were to manage their emotional problems, such events would be happening far too frequently to call them miracles.

Paul spells out the process through which healing most often comes to us in our battle with anger:

"Wherefore, my beloved, as ye have always obeyed, not as in my presence only, but now much more in my absence, work out your own salvation with fear and trembling. For it is God which worketh in you both to will and to do of his good pleasure" (Philippians 2:12,13, KJV).

Anger is a poor master—but a good servant!

Jesus directed the energy of His anger into His battle with the legalistic religion of the Pharisees. He held up to ridicule a religion that was more interested in seeing its rules kept than in helping people who hurt.

Remember, Jesus and the apostles directed the energy created during their angry moments into a project which gained for them the reputation of *"these that have turned the world upside down"* (Acts 17:6).

Multiply the productivity of your life. Convert the energy of your angry moments into activities which will bless God and benefit others. Do more than make a friend of your anger—*make it your servant and God's servant.*

Doing this will also resolve a major *guilt* issue for many believers. In the next chapter, you will learn how to tell the difference between *healthy guilt the Holy Spirit raises in your conscience* in order to keep you close to God and *unhealthy guilt the enemy uses* to falsely accuse you.

Chapter Five

Coming to Terms with Guilt
" 'The Me That Still Can Be' in Jesus"

One day when I came back to the office after lunch there was a message for me to return a call from a man on the east coast. As he began to talk, I could hear the anxiety in his voice. Fred was a young man still in his twenties. After the first few minutes of our conversation, I knew the nature of his problem even though I had not talked with him before.

He was obsessively preoccupied with obscenities directed toward God. He believed those obsessions constituted an unpardonable sin. (An obsession is an idea which persistently intrudes into a person's thought life and preoccupies that person.)

He saw himself beyond the reach of forgiveness. Because he had allowed himself to think these terrible things about God, he believed there was no hope for his salvation and that he was doomed to hell.

At EMERGE, we frequently see people with these particular obsessions. Such symptoms *seem to be* spiritual in nature, since they involve obscenities toward God. However, the purpose of symptoms in emotional disturbances is to distract the person's attention away from their real problem. Unfortunately, the symptoms usually create more pain and dissipate more energy than would be required to confront the underlying difficulty.

Fred's basic problem was emotional, not spiritual. He was suffering from unhealthy guilt, resulting in a need to condemn himself. Certainly, as an evangelical Christian, Fred's thoughts about God would give him all the evidence he needed to conclude that he had committed the "unpardonable sin," was the world's greatest sinner, and a rotten excuse for a human being.

What kind of unresolved problems in a person's past would result in such an exaggerated need to condemn himself? In most cases with similar symptoms, the person is struggling with guilt rooted in sexual violations of their conscience. Such unresolved sexual guilt usually stems from histories of masturbation, pornography, premarital sexual contacts, unconfessed adultery, bestiality, or abortion.

In view of this, you might think that the problem is basically a spiritual one, but it isn't. *The symptoms are religious, but the basic problem is rooted in the way these people feel and think about themselves.*

The problem is more emotional than spiritual.

When you ask people with Fred's problem if they have asked God to forgive them, usually they give one of two answers. Some will say they have asked God to forgive them many times, but they don't believe He has. Others will say they believe God has forgiven them, but they cannot forgive themselves.

In the first instance, the person is responding to his need to condemn himself by rejecting God's forgiveness. In the second, he refuses to forgive himself. In either event, he is fighting a losing battle with unhealthy guilt.

Basically, the problem is more emotional than spiritual. That is, *the issue is more within himself than between him and God.*

As you will discover later in this chapter, one of the distinguishing differences between healthy and unhealthy guilt is that *unhealthy guilt never yields to forgiveness,* regardless of how often one prays for it. The discerning believer knows that when this is the case, it is in direct contradiction to 1 John 1:9 (KJV):

"If we confess our sins, he is faithful and just to forgive us our sins, and to cleanse us from all unrighteousness."

God never visits unhealthy guilt on anyone.

When a person is afflicted with guilt which confession does not relieve, that guilt is self-imposed. The result is self-condemnation. This emotional need to condemn oneself becomes the primary target for treatment.

People who suffer from this type of problem are usually believers. Therefore, I have found a Biblical approach to their healing is more acceptable to them—and therefore more likely to be effective.

I arranged a series of appointments with Fred. As I had first suspected, I discovered he was suffering from unresolved sexual guilt. In his case, it was masturbatory guilt. Over 90 percent of young men and almost 40 percent of young women practice masturbation prior to marriage.

Lust . . . or a matter of private conscience?

Some young people do not feel guilty about masturbation. However, many do. For these people, masturbatory guilt poses a major mental health problem. Young people desperately need help in determining whether or not guilt is appropriate for them. But because the church is so divided over this matter, little or no help is to be found.

Matters which are critical to our salvation are specifically dealt with in Scripture. However, the practice of masturbation is not specifically discussed in the Bible. Therefore, the critical moral issue in masturbation is not the activity itself, but the nature of a person's fantasies during the activity. Pornographic or lustful fantasies are clearly condemned in Scripture. In Matthew 5:28 (KJV), Jesus says:

"Whosoever looketh on a woman to lust after her hath committed adultery with her already in his heart."

What is lust? Lust is the selfish use of another person for one's own pleasure. It can involve an actual person, pictures, sounds, or stories of persons. In any event, lust makes no commitment to another person. It assumes no responsibility for another person. It simply motivates a person to use or abuse others for their own selfish pleasure.

If the fantasy that preoccupies a person during masturbation is lustful, then guilt is the appropriate response of a healthy conscience. If a person prefers masturbation after marriage, they are in violation of 1 Corinthians 7:5 (NIV):

"Do not deprive each other except by mutual consent and for a time, so that you may devote yourselves to prayer. Then come together again so that Satan will not tempt you because of your lack of self-control."

When a single person's masturbatory fantasies center on what it will be like to celebrate the gift of sexuality in marriage, and he or she does not feel guilty about the practice, others should not attempt to bring this person into judgment. Fantasizing and dreaming about marriage while thinking sexual thoughts is a healthy way to manage one's sexuality. When this is the source of a single person's excitement, I choose to leave the matter of guilt to their private conscience—along with the other matters Paul deals with in the 14th chapter of Romans.

How does God deal with us about other sins?

Most of those who feel guilty about masturbation have been taught that God will not forgive them unless they quit. So they promise God that they will quit if He will forgive them. He forgives them, but they don't (or can't) quit. Since they are unable to quit, they assume that God has withdrawn His forgiveness.

Is this the way God deals with us about our other sins? If so, then we are all in trouble. Who among us can quit everything for which he needs to be forgiven? Have you quit everything for which you have ever been forgiven? Of course not. Neither have I. If God doesn't deal with us this way about other sins, why should such a special case be made of masturbation?

Such an approach is unsound *theologically* because it assumes forgiveness is based on our ability to stop a practice for which we feel guilty. Such a salvation then would be by our works, not by God's grace.

This approach is also unsound *psychologically,* because it creates an obsessive need to remember what it is you're not supposed to do. This keeps the subject on your mind—which preoccupies you with it and makes it much *more likely* that you will do it again.

As I explained this to Fred, I could hear relief in his voice. This was the first time in his life anyone had ever discussed this subject with him. Simply discovering that others had similar struggles helped him not to feel so odd about himself any more.

"What should I do when it happens again?" he asked.

"Well," I said, "what do you do when you *say things* again that you promised God you wouldn't *say* any more?"

115

"I ask God to forgive me," Fred replied.

"And you believe that He does," I reflected.

"Sure," Fred said confidently.

"How long have you been managing your verbal sins this way?" I asked.

"Ever since I've been a Christian," he answered.

"Why haven't you quit saying all those things you feel you shouldn't say?" I challenged.

"I want to," he said slowly. "I try."

"So, even though you haven't quit saying those things, God still forgives you as often as you ask Him because He knows *you want to quit* and *you are trying.* Do you suppose God would treat your problem with masturbation the same way He treats your problem with language?" I asked.

"I never thought of it that way before," Fred said. Reflecting for a moment, he finally answered, "I believe He would."

"So do I," I reassured him.

This became the basis of our treatment approach. Fred began to see that God was not condemning him. He was condemning himself. As he learned to bring this part of his life under the atonement, unhealthy guilt diminished. His preoccupation with obscenities toward God gradually disappeared. Today, he is married and enjoying an active place of Christian service in his local church.

Man's struggle with guilt runs throughout Scripture.

Adam and Eve hiding from God in the Garden of Eden . . . Cain trying to explain Abel's death to God . . . Noah drunk and naked . . . Abraham casting Hagar and Ishmael out of his home . . . Jacob wrestling all night with an angel . . . Joseph's brothers groveling before him when he was prime minister of Egypt . . .

Moses burying the Egyptian he had slain ... Achan stashing the Babylonian garment in his tent ... Samson waking in Delilah's lap with his hair cut off and his power gone ... David hearing Nathan's riddle ... the adulterous woman thrown down at Jesus' feet ... the Samaritan woman hearing Jesus review her marital history ... Judas bargaining for twenty pieces of silver ... Peter denying his Lord ... all of these characters of the Bible felt the pangs of the human family's common struggle with guilt.

You and I join this pathetic parade when we displease God, disappoint our family, or deny our better selves. The violation of one or more of these relationships is our most common source of healthy guilt.

Healthy guilt builds good character.

The pain of healthy guilt is God's way of calling our attention to boundaries that have been violated, so that they can be restored. These boundaries are defined and reinforced by the conscience.

Paul frequently addresses issues related to the conscience. In 1 Timothy 1:18-20, he tells Timothy about Hymenaeus and Alexander who *"made shipwreck of their faith"* because they failed to listen to their conscience. Then he urges Timothy to hold onto his good conscience.

The ability to respond to healthy guilt feelings by coming to terms with them honestly and resolving them in Biblical ways is essential to building the believer's character. Over time, a person's character is revealed by his attitudes and behavior. When you know someone over a period of years, you learn their attitudes and behaviors. Once you know the person's character, you can predict fairly accurately how that person will respond to different situations. Character is that observable . . . and that predictable.

117

People can act out of character.

Of course, once in a while, any of us can and will act out of character. That is, a person of bad character is capable of doing good things. A habitual thief and liar may help an elderly person home with his groceries, but that doesn't make the thief a person of good character.

On the other hand, once in a while, a person of good character may do some bad things. For example, someone whose character has been above reproach for years may misbehave over a brief period of time, but that doesn't necessarily change his basic character. This is difficult for some Christians to accept—either about themselves or others.

One of the tragedies of the church is that when good people have momentary lapses of character, the many faithful years they have invested in God's kingdom are so easily forgotten. There is a tendency to judge them harshly for behavior which is basically out of character for them.

Perhaps this is why Paul admonished the Galatians:

"Brethren, if a man be overtaken in a fault, ye which are spiritual, restore such an one in the spirit of meekness; considering thyself, lest thou also be tempted."
(Galatians 6:1, KJV)

The power of your conscience.

What makes your character so predictable? Your conscience. Your character is a product of your conscience.

The Bible talks about the relationship between conscience and character. Paul predicts:

"That in the latter times some shall depart from the faith, giving heed to seducing spirits, and doctrines of devils; Speaking lies in hypocrisy; having their conscience seared with a hot iron" (1 Timothy 4:1,2, KJV).

In 1 Timothy 1:18,19 (KJV), Paul reminds Timothy of the spiritual fate of those who abandon conscience:

"This charge I commit unto thee, son Timothy, according to the prophecies which went before on thee, that thou by them mightest war a good warfare; Holding faith, and a good conscience; which some having put away concerning faith have made shipwreck."

Where does your conscience come from?

God has given the capacity for conscience to every human being. Romans 2:14,15 (KJV) makes this clear:

"(For when the Gentiles, which have not the law, do by nature the things contained in the law, these, having not the law, are a law unto themselves: Which show the work of the law written in their hearts, their conscience also bearing witness, and their thoughts the mean while accusing or else excusing one another.)"

Your conscience is a divine mark which sets you off from brute beasts. Every normal person is born with the capacity for conscience. However, the content of your conscience (those things you consider right and wrong) is culturally derived. Therefore, the kinds of things for which each of us feels guilty will be greatly affected by the part of the world in which we were born and the part of the country in which we were raised.

For example, Americans eat beef—but those who live in Hindu countries would consider this to be a sacrilege. On the other hand, they might eat dog—which Americans would find most repulsive.

In the south, where I was raised, we were taught to address older people with respect. "Yes, ma'am." "No, ma'am." "Yes, sir." "No, sir." These were courtesies ingrained in my conscience as a child which I discovered didn't usually exist in the consciences

119

of children in Ohio, where we moved when I was in my teens. So, you see, your conscience is not only affected by the country in which you were born; it is also affected by the particular part of the country in which you were raised.

Who forms the conscience?

Your family forms your conscience. In Genesis 5:3 we are told that Adam had a son in his own likeness. Two things make this possible: (1) Genetic transmission, which selectively passes on to us the physical characteristics of our parents' families and perhaps more of their emotional and moral tendencies than we have suspected; and (2) Conscience formation, which is primarily responsible for the transmission of family character from one generation to another.

Specifically, our parents transmit our genetic inheritance to us and they form our conscience. Our spiritual heritage, transmitted largely through the conscience, is far more important than the physical characteristics we receive from our parents.

Three qualities of a good conscience . . .

One of the most valuable gifts you can receive from your parents is a good conscience. What is a good conscience? How do you define it? Here are three qualities by which a good conscience can be identified.

First of all, a good conscience is *neither too broad nor too narrow.* While it won't let you get away with too much, it also won't condemn you for too little. A good conscience will not let you be comfortable in breaking the law or offending the important relationships in your life.

Second, a good conscience is *consistent* in its vigilance. It grants its approval and imposes its sanctions regardless of time or place. It will not be conveniently silenced.

Third, a good conscience is *forgiving.* Once you respond to the pangs of a good conscience with confession and—if necessary—some form of restitution, it will no longer hurt you. It will let you be at peace with God and yourself.

How does a good conscience grow?

For a moment, let's look at how your conscience is formed. Conscience develops out of our interaction with our parents during the first five years of life. It emerges as parental love selectively alleviates infant fears. Initially, this interaction between parent and child centers largely around the amount of physical space given to us as infants.

The brain associates pain and pleasure with person and place. Any pediatrician will verify this observation. Pediatricians have done everything possible to make children less fearful in their offices. Most of them no longer wear a white coat in the office. They've have taken the medicinal odor away and surrendered their hypodermic syringes to their nurses. They provide little gifts for their patients. But as long as our infants get their immunization shots in that office, we can expect them to scream out their predictable protests when they enter.

Why? Because the brain associates pain with place. Regardless of how the pediatrician's "place" is neutralized, the child's brain warns him sooner or later he's going to get it "in the end."

The physical experiences of pain and pleasure become associated with the emotions of fear and love. We fear the places where we experience pain and we are fond of the places where we experience pleasure. This simple mechanism becomes the cradle of conscience.

You can give your child a healthy conscience.

By avoiding certain definable extremes and following a very simple three-step formula, parents can be assured they are giving their child a healthy conscience.

Let's look first at the extremes to be avoided. *Be sure the limits you set for your child are not too broad.* Allowing a child to jump up and down on the furniture and talk disrespectfully to adults is not in the child's best interests. Giving too much physical and emotional freedom produces a child other people can't stand. Later in life, such broad limits for the conscience leaves the child without the protection of painful proddings when values and ideals are about to be violated.

On the other hand, *avoid setting limits for the child which are too narrow.* This results in the child seeing you as being very difficult—if not impossible—to please. Often, having to deal with such narrow limits produces a guilt-prone child who is displeased with himself much of the time.

Inconsistent limits are the most devastating. A child subjected to this kind of environment is unsure how to feel about himself because he is unsure how his parents feel about him.

Now that we've looked at the extremes to be avoided, let me give you the simple formula we referred to earlier. You create a healthy conscience in your child when you set limits that are . . .

Fair.

Parents will often ask, "How do I know when my limits are fair?"

I simply reply, "Put yourself in your child's place. Then ask yourself how much liberty you could safely manage." This application of Christian compassion toward your child is one of the most practical ways I know to test the fairness of your limits.

Firm.

Firm, fair limits help to produce a sense of loving security in your child. From time to time, it's part of our fallen nature to test—and protest—any limits on our behavior. So, don't depend upon your child's pleasant acceptance of your limits to indicate their appropriateness. Remember how you protested your parents' limits, as a child. Any healthy person must learn to live within limits. The sooner in life we learn that, the better.

Friendly.

If your limits are fair, you should be able to enforce them firmly without feeling you are being cruel to your child. Unfortunately, some parents only know how to be firm when they are angry. Without knowing it, they are teaching their children to delay any compliance with their limits until the parent's voice reaches a certain level reflecting an unmistakable look of anger. "How many times have I told you? The answer is NO. Don't you understand that? It's spelled n-o. NO!"

This kind of harangue is not necessary. Remember what Paul says in Colossians 3:21 (KJV): *"Fathers, provoke not your children to anger, lest they be discouraged."*

Gently and firmly enforce your limits. "I'm sorry you feel so angry because I said you couldn't go. But it's my job to set the limits for you. It's your job to come to terms with them. All of your protests aren't going to change what I've decided, so why not get busy doing something that will take your mind off this?"

Such a response establishes the parent's control and it also helps the youngster learn how to accept limits without being too preoccupied by their frustration.

How healthy is your conscience?

As a parent, how healthy is your conscience? What are the things that make you feel guilty? A healthy conscience will impose guilt when you are engaging in behavior which endangers your life, your character, or your property; or the life, character, or property of someone else.

Once conscience is formed, it is highly resistant to change. For most of us, this is a blessing. We have had loving parents who have given us a healthy conscience. Even after we have established our own personal faith in Christ, we do not have to struggle with a faulty conscience.

Once we become Christians, our conscience has to be Scripturally re-trained so that it is sensitive to limits placed upon the believer's behavior by the Bible. However, once this has been done, the conscience continues to be a consistent monitor of our behavior—rewarding us when we obey Christ's teaching and reprimanding us when we disobey. A healthy conscience plays a prominent role in determining the extent to which Christ is reflected in our attitudes and behavior.

How to treat a sick conscience . . .

The resistance of the conscience to change presents some Christians with an urgent need for spiritual healing. Their consciences are unhealthy. If you find yourself in this group, here is an A-B-C formula to help you begin retraining your conscience to feel healthy guilt.

A. Acknowledge your need for healing in this area of your life.

How do you know if you need healing for your conscience? Look carefully at the role guilt has played in your past. Some people come into the kingdom of God with lives characterized by a lack of discipline. They have been dominated by habits, attitudes, and behaviors which have demonstrated a callous disregard of others in their own pursuit of pleasure. All of this has precipitated little—if any—guilt in them.

These people need to have their consciences narrowed and strengthened to help them be more sensitive to the ways their attitudes and behaviors contradict Scripture and bring unnecessary pain into the lives of others. Unfortunately, people with this problem seldom seek help for themselves. When we see them in clinical practice it is usually because their attitudes and behaviors have brought others such pain that some kind of treatment is demanded.

Among our treatment population we are much more likely to find Christians who are suffering from a conscience which is too narrow. Since this problem is so pervasive among believers, I have chosen to give it special attention later in the chapter.

B. Believe that God can help you correct a faulty conscience.

After all, if God can make you His child, He can do anything. If He can perform the miracle of regeneration in us, then certainly He can heal a sick conscience. The Bible provides us with beautiful examples of this.

First of all, let's look at Jacob. His conscience was too broad. He bought his brother's birthright and stole his brother's blessing without experiencing enough guilt to make him see how wrong this was.

In Genesis chapter 32, God tells us about Jacob's all-night wrestling match with the angel of the Lord. This spiritual battle brought healing to Jacob's conscience. From that time on, Jacob experienced too much emotional pain to continue his devious ways. The God who changed Jacob's character from that of a deceiver (which is what "Jacob" meant) to a person who had power with God (which is what his new name, "Israel," meant) can still touch a person and help them change both their conscience and their character.

Second, there was Mary Magdalene. Before she met Jesus, there is no indication she suffered guilt for earning her living as a prostitute. However, when she came to Christ, He healed her conscience and changed her character.

Third, Paul underwent a real transformation of conscience when he became a Christian. Until that time he was a Pharisee and was driven by a hard, unyielding conscience. He was a legalist of the legalists. Here's how he pictured himself:

"If any other man thinketh that he hath whereof he might trust in the flesh, I more: Circumcised the eighth day, of the stock of Israel, of the tribe of Benjamin, an Hebrew of the Hebrews; as touching the law, a Pharisee; Concerning zeal, persecuting the church; touching the righteousness which is in the law, blameless" (Philippians 3:4–6, KJV).

Can you imagine what a harsh, judgmental conscience Saul of Tarsus must have had before Christ touched him? Yet, sometime after his conversion and before he wrote his first letter to the Corinthian church, a miracle of inner healing took place in Paul's life. He describes the transformation which the healing brought to his life in this way:

"For though I be free from all men, yet have I made myself servant unto all, that I might gain the more. And unto the Jews I became as a Jew, that I might gain the Jews; to them that are under the law, as under the law, that I might gain them that are under the law; to them that are without law, as without law, (being not without law to God, but under the law to Christ,) that I might gain them that are without law. To the weak became I weak, that I might gain the weak: I am made all things to all men, that I might by all means save some" (1 Corinthians 9:19–22, KJV).

What tremendous flexibility is now evident in this old Pharisee's conscience! How did such a psychological miracle happen? The Jesus who transformed his life also healed his conscience—and changed his character.

C.   Concentrate your spiritual efforts.

Work on any transformation of conscience you may need until the necessary correction is made. Your spiritual life will only be as healthy as your conscience. So, keep working at it!

Healthy vs. unhealthy guilt.

The person who will have the greatest struggle in his battle for a healthy conscience is the one whose conscience is too narrow and rigid. Often, such people are afraid they won't feel guilty enough to be saved. Their conscience is a tyrant.

They will need to learn the difference between healthy and unhealthy guilt if they are ever to overthrow the impossible yoke of such a tyrannical conscience. Let's take a look at three characteristics which define that difference for you.

1. **Unhealthy guilt is rooted in rules; healthy guilt is rooted in relationships.**

I grew up around a religion of rules. Unfortunately, I can't remember as much attention being focused upon a violation of relationships as on breaking the rules.

It was against the rules to play on Sunday. Even during the week, we couldn't play the "Old Maid" card game unless we closed the drapes first—to be sure we wouldn't be a stumbling block to someone who might look through the windows and think we were "playing cards."

I was afraid to play a pinball machine because if Christ were to return or if I should die before I had a chance to repent, my salvation could be in jeopardy.

The Christians in Galatia were prone to this kind of legalism. Even though Paul brought them out from such bondage, persuasive teachers attempted to put them under the bondage of the law again. That's why Paul wrote to them:

"Stand fast therefore in the liberty wherewith Christ hath made us free, and be not entangled again with the yoke of bondage ... For, brethren, ye have been called unto liberty; only use not liberty for an occasion to the flesh, but by love serve one another. For all the law is fulfilled in one

word, even in this; Thou shalt love thy neighbor as thyself. But if ye bite and devour one another, take heed that ye be not consumed of one another" (Galatians 5:1,13–15, KJV).

A legalistic faith tends to make judges out of believers. In such a frame of mind it is easy to be more concerned about keeping rules than maintaining relationships. Unhealthy guilt will preoccupy you with concern for rules and allow you to neglect your relationships.

Healthy guilt inflicts pain to warn you that important relationships in your life are being threatened by your attitudes and behaviors. The Pharisees were concerned that Jesus keep their rules, but He was more concerned about the state of their relationships with God.

Take time to survey the important relationships in your life. How healthy are they? What is the state of your relationship with God? How much of yourself have you invested in the interest of healthy family relationships? Who are your closest friends? Are you caring for those relationships?

These are the vital issues of your life. A healthy conscience will force you to face them honestly. When you are neglecting these relationships, a good conscience will cause you enough emotional pain to bring these matters to your attention. When you address them responsibly, a healthy conscience will not only reward you with relief; it will also give you the kind of commendation which leaves you feeling good about the priorities of your life.

2. **Both healthy and unhealthy guilt carry with them a compulsion to confess.**

The key to distinguishing the difference between healthy and unhealthy guilt is in the kinds of things you are being driven to confess. Honestly ask yourself whether the issues being raised by your conscience are vital to a healthy relationship with God and with the people who are important to you.

Remember, Jesus identified the Pharisees' consciences as unhealthy because they could not distinguish the difference between rules and relationships. Or, as He put it, they couldn't tell the difference between a "speck of sawdust" and a "plank," betweena "gnat" and a "camel," or the inside versus the outside of a cup or dish.

"Why do you look at the speck of sawdust in your brother's eye and pay no attention to the plank in your own eye?" (Matthew 7:3, NIV).

"Woe to you, teachers of the law and Pharisees, you hypocrites! You give a tenth of your spices— mint, dill, and cumin. But you have neglected the more important matters of the law—justice, mercy, and faithfulness. You should have practiced the latter, without neglecting the former. You blind guides! You strain out a gnat but swallow a camel.

"Woe to you, teachers of the law and Pharisees, you hypocrites! You clean the outside of the cup and dish, but inside they are full of greed and self-indulgence. Blind Pharisees! First clean the inside of the cup and dish, and then the outside also will be clean.

"Woe to you, teachers of the law and Pharisees, you hypocrites! You are like whitewashed tombs, which look beautiful on the outside but on the inside are full of dead men's bones and everything unclean. In the same way, on the outside you appear to people as righteous but on the inside you are full of hypocrisy and wickedness."

(Matthew 23:23-28)

3.   **Unhealthy guilt never yields to forgiveness, but healthy guilt always does.**

I often ask people suffering from unhealthy guilt, "What is it that you've done to prompt this awful, unrelenting guilt?" Most often they simply respond that they don't know what they've done to cause it.

Many of these people tell of long sessions of prayer during which they beg God to show them what is wrong in their life. As soon as someone tells me this, I know their guilt is not from God. God always lets us know exactly why He is making us feel guilty. You and I may hold things against each other without revealing what's wrong, but God is not like that.

Husbands and wives are likely to play these kinds of games with each other. What couple hasn't headed home from some social gathering with the wife seated so far from her husband that if it weren't for the car door, she would be outside the car?

Can't you just hear—or repeat—the conversation?

He says, "What's wrong, honey? What did I do? What did I say? Why are you so upset and sitting so far over on your side?" And he's really not sure what he's done.

Her arms are folded tightly and the look on her face could wilt a plastic flower. She answers, "If you don't know, I'm not going to tell you!"

Husbands are just as capable of playing this game. In a similar situation, the man roars out of the driveway on two wheels instead of four, peels rubber as he heads down the street, and fills the car with eloquent, stony silence. His wife, attempting to relieve the situation, says something like, "I know I must have done something wrong, dear. But what did I do? What did I say? What's wrong?"

From the driver's seat, his jaw clenched, comes her husband's thundering response: "You know what's wrong!

A person suffering from unhealthy guilt thinks God is like that pouting wife or that angry husband. He thinks he has to beg

God to tell him the source of his guilt. Nothing could be farther from the truth!

If the guilt you experience is from God, He will be specific in identifying the source as soon as you ask Him. God does not play games with us. The only reason the Holy Spirit ever inflicts the pain of guilt is to safeguard your relationship with God and the important people in your life.

The purpose of divine conviction is to bring you to the place of forgiveness. As soon as corrective actions are taken in your attitudes and behavior to remove any threat to important life relationships, the pain God inflicts upon you will be lifted.

Remember what the Scriptures say:

"If we confess our sins, he is faithful and just to forgive us our sins and to cleanse us from all unrighteousness."
(1 John 1:9, KJV)

Guilt that remains after you've honestly confessed your sins to Jesus Christ is the work of a sick conscience. It is tragic to see people insist on punishing themselves for a mistake in their past. They seem to believe that their willingness to suffer somehow impresses God with the sincerity of their remorse. However, Jesus died for our sins. It is sacrilege to suggest that any pain I inflict upon myself could add to the atonement purchased by His death.

Don't worship the idol of "the me that might have been."

When Evelyn first came to see me, she was in her 40s. She was anxious, angry, and guilty. Evelyn had been on tranquilizers for years.

After each of her first few sessions, she would say, "I know there's something I have to tell you if I am going to get better, but I just don't have the courage. I'm afraid you'll lose all respect for me once you know."

131

I reassured her that it was highly unlikely she could tell me anything I hadn't heard many times before. However, her secret had accumulated so much anxiety through the years that she simply could not bear facing it.

Finally, she opened a session by announcing, "This is the day. I made up my mind to get this whole business out of me today." This was her story.

When Evelyn was a teenager, she became sexually involved with a young man from her church. Unfortunately, she conceived. When it became obvious that she was pregnant, the pastor forced her and the young man to get up in front of a crowded sanctuary and confess that they had sinned. By that time, Evelyn's condition was apparent to everyone.

In spite of this humiliation, Evelyn and her boyfriend stayed in the church. They married and, with the help of their families, they began to build a stable marriage. To spare their first child (Margie) all the embarrassment they could, they managed to have the date on her birth certificate changed. Other children were born to the marriage.

Through the years, Evelyn and her husband became respected members of the community and leaders in their church. However, Evelyn's sick conscience continued to inflict pain on her over this unfortunate mistake of her youth.

Evelyn's best friend, in whom she had confided during the trying weeks of her first pregnancy, moved away shortly after Margie was born. A few months before Evelyn came to see me, this woman's husband was transferred back into the area.

Evelyn's youngest daughter, Becky, and her friend's youngest daughter had developed a close relationship. Evelyn's big fear was that this woman would feel a moral obligation to tell Becky the story of Margie's conception. There were moments

132

when Evelyn knew her friend would never do this. However, much of the time she was tormented with this fear.

Once Evelyn had told me the entire story, I said, "Is that all?" Then she began to cry.

"You ask if that's all," she sobbed. "Isn't that enough?"

I reassured her. "Evelyn," I said, "I've heard very similar stories from many, many young women. Did you ask the Lord to forgive you at the time?"

"Oh, yes," she sobbed. "I asked God to forgive me then, and I've asked Him a hundred times or more since then."

"Do you believe He has forgiven you?" I asked.

"Of course I believe God has forgiven me," she answered, "but how can I ever forgive myself?"

As I became aware of the tremendous toll this unhealthy guilt had extracted from Evelyn's life, I became angry at the enemy. Just as Jesus said (John 10:10), Satan—the thief—had *stolen* years of emotional peace from this child of God. I felt anger in my voice as I said, "Oh; the blood of Jesus is adequate to satisfy God's holy nature, but it's not good enough for your holy conscience. Is that what you're saying? Must God send another Son to die for your holy conscience? Isn't one Calvary enough?"

By this time Evelyn was sobbing uncontrollably. I heard her say, through her tears, "My God, I've never seen it like that before." That day she realized she had unconsciously been trying to suffer enough to atone for her own sins. She had forgotten what Isaiah said:

"But he was wounded for our transgressions, he was bruised for our iniquities; the chastisement of our peace was upon him, and with his stripes we are healed."
(Isaiah 53:5, KJV)

133

God healed Evelyn that day. Her medical doctor began to withdraw her from prescription tranquilizers upon her next visit to his office. I saw her for periodic follow-up visits for the next several months.

The healing that came to her that day could have been hers years before. All the guilt she had needlessly inflicted upon herself was borne by Christ for all of us.

There's something insidious about a person like Evelyn being unable to forgive herself. Usually, such people are the last ones in the world to think of themselves as idolaters, but they *are* worshiping an idol. How many times do you suppose such people have said to themselves: "Oh, if only it hadn't happened that way. How different my life might have been. But my whole life is ruined now."

These people are worshiping the idol of "the me that might have been." Because "the me that might have been" can never be, they refuse to accept "the me that is." And since they won't accept "the me that is," they can't discover " 'the me that still can be' in Jesus."

Such an attitude toward life is like that of a little girl who has dropped her china doll and broken it. Her mother has picked it up and carefully mended it, but the little girl refuses to take it back because she knows it has a crack in it. Instead of focusing on the fact that she has her doll back, she keeps her eyes glued on the crack. Her doll is her idol. And all she can see is its flaw.

When you won't forgive yourself for some mistake in your past, you're really making an idol out of "the me that might have been." If you will smash that idol you've created and forgive yourself, God will help you discover " 'the me that still can be' in Jesus." Only as you let go of the past can you reach the future that can be yours.

134

Some people find this such a battle that they spend much of their life depressed. This kind of situational depression is very different from biochemical depression. In the next chapter, I will give you some ways to identify these two kinds of depression and share some suggestions for dealing with each.

Chapter Six

Dealing with Depression

As God's child, your best days are in your future!

Whenever I help a person deal with depression, it's more than just a clinical task for me. I remember how my first wife struggled with depression fairly early in our marriage. Shortly after she gave Caesarean section birth to our first child, she suffered a serious postpartum depression.

I knew she loved God. Her consistent daily devotional life told me that. And yet, this was something apart from her spiritual life that she just couldn't deal with.

She recalled this as a time in her life when she had no conscious awareness of God's presence. She believed that our newborn son and I would be better off without her. For six months she wanted to die. On three different occasions she tried to take her life. For several months after her last suicide attempt, life was *still* a world of deep valleys and dark skies for her.

There is no way to describe the powerlessness and helplessness I experienced. I sought every way humanly possible to be of some help to her, only to discover that nothing seemed to work. However, I did learn the importance of allowing her to express her feelings to me. And, even though she couldn't believe in her recovery, I never allowed *myself* to doubt it would happen. I'm happy to say God eventually healed her. And out of the pain of that experience, I was driven to the Scriptures to study what they had to say about mental health issues—and depression in particular. I was surprised to discover how many people in Scripture suffered from depression, and the ways God helped them deal with it. I think you will be, too.

In this chapter we are going to focus on four questions people frequently ask about depression: *What is depression? Who suffers from it? What are its symptoms? How can a person deal with it?*

What is depression?

Depression, as a form of human suffering, has been around for a very long time. In fact, it is probably as old as the first moments after Adam and Eve tasted of the forbidden fruit. Depression is the most common form of emotional pain. It is so common, in fact, that most of us will have to learn how to come to terms with it at some time in our life.

Hippocrates, the father of modern medicine, gave us our first clinical definition of depression in the fourth century B.C. He identified it as the "black humour," which he called "melancholia."

Today, the National Association for Mental Health defines depression as:

An emotional state of dejection and sadness, ranging from mild discouragement and downheartedness to feelings of utter hopelessness and despair.

Such a clinical definition of depression lacks the human element for those who have experienced it. If you have known the pain of depression, you have a far more realistic understanding of it than can ever be put into words.

Abraham Lincoln wrote, "If what I feel were equally distributed to the whole human family, there would not be one cheerful face on earth."

The "age of depression."

Researchers refer to our day as the "age of depression," and for good reasons. Since World War II, each successive generation of Americans has shown higher rates of depression. Today, young people in their teens and twenties are *ten times more likely* to suffer from major depression than were their grandparents fifty years ago. Consequently, suicide is the second highest cause of death among teenagers. Accidental deaths (including auto accidents) are the leading cause of teen deaths, and there is no way to know how many of these accidents are disguised suicides.

As strange as it may seem, the old and very old in our society are at much lower risk for depression than are the young. For females, the average age of onset for major depression is 15-19. For males, it is 25-29. Private physicians report that as many as 48 percent of their patients suffer from some form of depression.

What are the symptoms of depression?

The symptoms of depression vary with the intensity. Most of us experience "the blues" from time to time. The zest goes out of our life. We feel sad and dejected. We may retreat into temporary silence and reflect a surly mood.

These normal "downs" of life generally last only a day or two. As a rule of thumb, our therapists tell people to accept any depression that doesn't last longer than four or five days as a normal bout with "the blues." Any depression that lasts much longer than four days should be given careful attention.

139

As depression deepens, physiological processes tend to become involved. A person may experience an eating disorder. Sleep disturbance is common: difficulty going to sleep, interrupted sleep, and early awakening are often reported. A person's normal sex drive wanes or temporarily disappears.

When depression is primarily a product of disturbed biochemistry, frequently one or both of the following symptoms appear:

1.   The person exhibits "pervasive anhedonia."

This is a total absence of pleasure. Nothing makes this person happy or brightens their mood. They can hear that one of their loved ones, for whom they have prayed for years, has come to Christ—and give no evidence of joy. They can learn that they have suddenly become wealthy, and exhibit no emotional response. Their sense of humor is gone. *They are incapable of pleasure.* Knowing this can save you the frustration of trying to cheer them up.

2.   The person presents an unresponsive mood.

A *normal* person reacts emotionally to the mood of whatever group he is with. Even a *situationally depressed* person can be cheered up temporarily by the people around him. However, many *biochemically depressed* people remain impassive and oblivious to the mood of their social environment.

The *most serious symptom* of depression is the presence of *suicidal wishes.* Contrary to popular opinion, people who commit suicide *do* talk about it. In fact, it is rare for someone to commit suicide without making that intention known in some way.

If any member of your family seriously thinks about or talks about committing suicide, the safest thing you can do is get them to a professional person who can measure the suicidal risk.

If your loved one needs to be hospitalized for his own protection, urge him to consent to it. If he won't, take whatever legal steps may be required to give him the protection he needs. It is better to tolerate his protests to hospitalization than to live with the regret of any negligence on your part.

In the vast majority of cases, if the depressed person can be given the protection he needs during the most despairing time of his illness, he will survive. A chronically suicidal person eventually may succeed in taking his life, but as a family member or mental health professional, I want to be sure I have taken every step I can to prevent it.

What does depression "look like" on a person? What do our counselors see that tells them a person is depressed? Here is a typical cluster of symptoms:

1. *A depressed mood—the helplessness-hopelessness syndrome.*

2. *Loss of pleasure or interest in usual activities.*

3. *Disturbance of appetite—which may show up as anorexia (severe loss of appetite) or bulimia (binge eating followed by the use of laxatives or forced vomiting).*

4. *Sleep disturbance.*

5. *Marked increase or decrease in level of physical activity or "motion."*

6. *Loss of energy.*

7. *Feelings of worthlessness and guilt.*

8. *Difficulty thinking or concentrating; indecisiveness.*

9. *Recurrent thoughts of death and/or suicide.*

The appearance of these symptoms identifies a depressed person. Requesting prayer from Christian friends and reporting

141

the symptoms to your family physician should bring welcome relief from the symptoms of less serious forms of depression. Deeper, more serious depression will no doubt require professional intervention.

Who suffers from depression?

Among church people, there seems to be a widespread but mistaken notion that emotional suffering of any kind is inconsistent with the Christian faith. However, *everybody* is subject to mental health problems. If you haven't had any yet, be grateful!

When a believer experiences a major bout with depression, he is often suspected of hiding some dark sin in his life. Somehow, believers are expected by many of their peers to live above all forms of discouragement or depression.

I remember the unnecessary pain this particular point of view caused my wife and me while we were going through her difficult postpartum depression. I say "we" because when your mate is seriously depressed, you are also affected by it.

We were young evangelists. We couldn't find a pastor who understood our mental health problem. And we couldn't find a mental health professional who respected our faith.

Our Christian friends advised, "Just get her into the Word and pray." Mental health professionals said, "Your religion is what's making your wife mentally ill. Look at her symptoms. She believes she has committed some unpardonable sin. Get her out of her crazy religion." Many people suffer from unnecessarily narrow points of view like these.

A healthy faith can alleviate many of the anxieties and tensions of the mentally ill. On the other hand, Christians can also benefit from the competent care of a mental health professional who respects their faith. It is gratifying to see more and more pastors and mental health professionals discover this.

I knew my wife's suffering was not due to any neglect of prayer and Scripture reading. She was spending twice as much time in these exercises as I was—and I wasn't depressed! I also knew her faith was too important a part of her life for her to be helped by abandoning it. She needed the support of a healthy faith *and* competent mental health care.

Job was depressed.

Even a casual reading of Scripture reveals that many devout believers have suffered the agony of deep depression.The oldest book of the Bible tells us how depressed Job was. Tornados had blown down his buildings and killed his children. Thieves had stolen his herds. His health was gone. He was a mass of sores from his head to his feet. He had lost everything. Neither his wife nor his friends understood his agony.

Job was so overwhelmed by his sense of loss that he withdrew into seven days of silence:

"Then they sat on the ground with him for seven days and seven nights. No one said a word to him, because they saw how great his suffering was" (Job 2:13, NIV).

Can you imagine being so depressed as to sit for seven days without uttering a word? He cursed the day he was born and wished he were dead:

"After this, Job opened his mouth and cursed the day of his birth. He said, 'May the day of my birth perish, and the night it was said, "A boy is born!" That day—may it turn to darkness; may God above not care about it; may no light shine upon it ...Why did I not perish at birth and die as I came from the womb?' " (Job 3:1-4,11, NIV).

His wife, not knowing any other way to offer him comfort, said to Job:

"Are you still holding on to your integrity? Curse God and die!" (Job 2:9, NIV).

Remember, now, this was the man God had bragged about to Satan:

*"Then the L*ORD *said to Satan, "Have you considered my servant Job? There is no one on earth like him; he is blameless and upright, a man who fears God and shuns evil"* (Job 1:8, NIV).

He was literally the best man in the world. If such a man as Job was depressed, certainly you and I have no reason to feel guilty when we get depressed. And in our depression, we have no difficulty understanding how Job felt when he said what he did. Those same kinds of thoughts have rushed through our heads.

David got depressed.

Even a casual reading of Psalm 42 (NIV) tells you David was depressed when he wrote it. Listen to some of the things he said:

"My tears have been my food day and night, while men say to me all day long, 'Where is your God?' " (v. 3).

"Why are you downcast, O my soul? Why so disturbed within me? Put your hope in God, for I will yet praise him, my Savior and my God. My soul is downcast within me; therefore will I remember you from the land of the Jordan, the heights of Hermon—from Mount Mizar" (v. 5,6).

"I say to God my rock, 'Why have you forgotten me? Why must I go about mourning, oppressed by the enemy?' My bones suffer mortal agony as my foes taunt me, saying to me all day long, 'Where is your God?' " (v. 9,10).

Elijah was also depressed.

Elijah was another great man of God who battled with depression. There was no doubt about the power he had with God. He had called fire down from heaven one day and rain another day. He had slaughtered the prophets of Baal. Yet, right in the middle of this spiritual high, depression struck. He found himself sitting under a juniper tree bemoaning his life and wishing he were dead.

"Elijah was afraid and ran for his life. When he came to Beersheba in Judah, he left his servant there, while he himself went a day's journey into the desert. He came to a broom tree, sat down under it, and prayed that he might die. 'I have had enough, LORD,' he said. 'Take my life; I am no better than my ancestors'" (1 Kings 19:3,4, NIV).

In the midst of his doldrums, Elijah became so paranoid that he began to believe he was the only prophet in all Israel who was true to God. Elijah complained:

"I have been very zealous for the LORD God Almighty. The Israelites have rejected your covenant, broken down your altars, and put your prophets to death with the sword. I am the only one left, and now they are trying to kill me too" (1 Kings 19:10).

God had to confront him after such an exaggeration and remind him:

"Yet I reserve seven thousand in Israel—all whose knees have not bowed down to Baal and all whose mouths have not kissed him" (1 Kings 19:18, NIV).

Another depressed prophet: Jonah!

After Jonah had preached such a powerful sermon that the whole city of Nineveh was converted, he became so depressed that he sat down under a temporary shelter he had made and prayed for God to take his life (Jonah 4:1-8).

You see, anyone can suffer from depression and, at some time in life, most people do. No depth of spirituality nor degree of perfection makes you immune from depression. The fact that you may need to seek professional help for relief from this pain does not reflect negatively on your relationship with God. If medication is needed, you should be able to take it with no more guilt than if you were fighting an infection.

What causes depression?

Depression is often a secondary symptom of physical illness. That is why a competent professional person will want you to have a physical examination before assuming that your depression is psychologically induced. If there is some physical problem, it is important that it be treated. Often, the successful treatment of your physical problem remedies your depression.

Just being a member of our modern society makes you a candidate for depression. If you can take the pace of life today without ever getting depressed, thank God and know that you are unusual. Most of us have our "down" times.

A serious loss can trigger a depression.

This kind of situational depression may follow the death of a loved one, a divorce, or bankruptcy. It can also be precipitated by the loss of a lover, a friend, or a job. The loss of the ability to bear children depresses some women. Often, both men and women experience depression upon retirement.

Depression can come from painful circumstances in life: marital tension, personal illness, parent-child conflict, work aggravations, business reverses, boredom, frustration with friends, or parental insensitiveness. Each of us has his share of these dilemmas also.

Often, the type of depression that is triggered by major change or loss may be referred to as a grief reaction. People experiencing grief reactions move through four predictable stages as they work their way toward wholeness again:

1. Shock.

This stage lasts from several hours to a few days. During this time, the person is dazed. What they are going through seems to be a bad dream or a nightmare. They expect to wake up and find out it isn't true. But they are awake . . . and it is true.

2. Storm.

This stage lasts from several days to several weeks and is characterized by emotional turbulence and upheaval. Anxiety, fear, hostility, and rage surge within the person at almost unbearable levels. This is the most painful period of recovery from a serious loss.

3. Search.

Once a person comes through the storm, he begins a search to find some meaning or purpose in this loss. Where is God in all of this? After all, the events of the loss, as tragic as they may be, are not what the person lives with; *he lives with his memory of the events.* Events do not repeat themselves, but memories do.

When we are going through these times it is easy to add to our discomfort by adopting unnecessarily distorted and exaggerated views of the situation. This is why it is so important that one allows God to provide a redemptive and healing purpose for the loss. The search should not end until such a meaning is found.

This is one area where our Christian faith will be severely tested by the enemy. He will tempt us to ask, "Why has God let this happen to me?" The answer to this question is that we live in a world where man has freedom of choice to act . . . and we sometimes have to live with the consequences of our own and others' thoughtless choices. The most obvious example of this is the pain of those families who lose an innocent family member because someone, somewhere, chose to drink alcohol and then drive.

Losses may come from acts of nature. Sometimes they come from illness. Sometimes they are indeed the result of our own behavior. *They are not, however, acts of God.* This is a very important thing to remember.

The question we need to ask ourselves is not, "Why has God let this happen to me?" Instead, we should be asking ourselves, "How can I find God in my tragedy? What can I learn about His sustaining love and grace as He goes with me through this?"

4.   Sequel.

There *is* life after the loss, although the nature of life in the sequel will never be the same. The quality of life after a major loss is determined largely by the person's resolution of the storm and their willingness to search for a redemptive purpose. This is a difficult task and one that is not accomplished quickly . . . but it is a necessary part of the healing process.

A learned negative view of life can cause depression.

Unfortunately, some people adopt a negative view of themselves and their world very early in life—long before they even start to school. It's not their circumstances which depress them; it's their view of life.

From childhood, they have viewed other people more favorably than themselves. Their value judgments are predictably negative. They are overly critical of themselves and others. They see what is wrong rather than what is right. If you showed them a donut, they would see the hole.

Once I saw a cartoon of an old western town. There was a banner over the main street bearing the name of the place: "Donut Center." Underneath the name, some kids had scrawled, "What a hole!" It is this kind of person who lives there. All of us may spend a few days of our lives in such a place now and then, but no one has to become a permanent resident.

As you journey through life, let this be your goal:
Keep your eye on the donut, and not on the hole!

Here are some suggestions for dealing with depression:

**1.   Don't let the fact that you're depressed
get you down!**

Fear of depression or guilt over being depressed will only add to your discomfort. Remember, depression tends to feed upon itself. You can become more depressed by dwelling on the fact that you are depressed already. Try not to make a big production out of your depression. Assure yourself that a few weeks—or, at the most a few months—will see you through it.

**2.   If you haven't had a thorough physical examination
in the past six months, get one.**

Even if nothing significant is found, at least you know that your depression is not symptomatic of some physical illness.

3.   Learn the therapy that comes from staying busy.

Unless your depression is severe, stay busy. Don't brood! You may not be able to escape your depression entirely, but it is not something you want to feed. Once you start to feed depression, you will discover it has a ravenous appetite. The more you feed it, the bigger it grows. So, the worst thing a depressed person can do is to brood. When you can, resist the temptation to dawdle and daydream. Plunge yourself into activities.

**4.   Discover the relief that comes from sharing your
burden with the Lord in prayer.**

David learned this secret centuries ago. In Psalm 55:22 (KJV), he wrote, *"Cast thy burden upon the LORD, and he shall sustain thee."*

Take time to read Psalms 58 and 59. Notice how openly David shared his feelings with the Lord. He said it just like he felt it.

Prayer can be a therapeutic way of venting anger.

For David, prayer became a therapeutic way of venting his anger and bitterness. He cried:

> *"Break their teeth, O God, in their mouth: break out the great teeth of the young lions, O Lord. Let them melt away as waters which run continually: when he bendeth his bow to shoot his arrows, let them be as cut in pieces. As a snail which melteth, let every one of them pass away."*
>
> (Psalm 58:6–8, KJV)

Can you imagine the relief that came to David as he emptied these feelings out before the Lord?

In Psalm 59, feeling overwhelmed by his enemies, he expressed his anxiety over his future. He made no attempt to cover up his bitterness and contempt as he prayed:

> *"Deliver me from the workers of iniquity, and save me from bloody men . . . They return at evening: they make a noise like a dog, and go 'round about the city. Behold, they belch out with their mouth . . . For the sin of their mouth and the words of their lips let them even be taken in their pride: and for cursing and lying which they speak. Consume them in wrath, consume them, that they may not be: and let them know that God ruleth in Jacob unto the ends of the earth"* (Psalm 59:2,6,7,12,13, KJV).

Learn to entrust your bitter, angry, hostile feelings to God. There is nothing you can feel that you can't express to Him in prayer. Find a private time and place for pouring out your heart before God.

Never fear that honestly disclosing your deepest feelings to God will alienate you from Him. You may have found it necessary to hide certain things from your parents when you were growing up, but there is nothing you cannot share with your heavenly Father. David's courage to be transparent with his feelings in prayer endeared him to God as a man after God's own heart (Acts 13:22). God longs for that kind of relationship with you, one which finds you *"casting all your care upon him; for he careth for you"* (1 Peter 5:7, KJV).

5.   Share your burden with a friend.

Talking helps. My heart goes out to people who grew up in homes where children were to be seen and not heard. As adults, they are likely to be very private people who keep their problems to themselves. They tried talking when they were younger, but no one wanted to listen. So, now they are convinced that talking doesn't help. But it does. Let me prove it to you.

Suppose you and three of your friends get in your car and head home after a night of fellowship. You approach the highway and make your entry safely. You start down the road. At the first major intersection, someone darts out in front of you. You have to swerve off the road to miss him. You almost have a wreck.

What are the chances that you and your friends will proceed homeward without some comment? Remember, there is no intellectual need to discuss it. You are all intelligent adults. Each of you saw everything that happened. None of you can add to the others' information.

However, I'll venture that you wouldn't get a quarter-mile down the road until one of you would ask, excitedly, "Did you see that idiot?" From an intellectual point of view, that is an absurd question. Of course, everyone in the car saw "that idiot."

However, before that question could be answered, someone else would be likely to observe, "Wow! We almost got it!"

It's highly likely that you would continue to talk about your close call all the way down the road together. And one of the first things each of you would probably say to the family as you

151

arrived home was, "We almost didn't get home. We could have all been killed."

Why carry on all this conversation if talking doesn't help? Well, the truth of the matter is, talking does help. It helps to reduce our level of anxiety. It helps to lighten our burden. That's why Paul instructs us, *"Bear ye one another's burdens, and so fulfill the law of Christ"* (Galatians 6:2, KJV).

A pastor friend of mine reminds couples of this important function of communication in marriage. Sometime during their marriage ceremony he reminds each couple that their close communication can "double life's joys" and "divide life's sorrows in half" as they share both life's pleasures and its pain with one another.

When words are used as God intends, they indeed decrease our pain and increase our pleasure. Healthy conversation within yourself and between you and a trusted friend can go a long way toward shortening the night of your depression and hastening the dawn of the new day you so long to see.

Surviving deep depression.

When depression is severe, a person may have to be temporarily relieved of all responsibilities. Notice how God treated Elijah's depression. He even put him in his own private hospital. The treatment God gave Elijah for deep depression is still sound. You can read about the regimen in 1 Kings 19:5-8 (KJV):

"And as he lay and slept under a juniper tree, behold, an angel touched him, and said unto him, Arise and eat. And he looked, and behold, there was a cake baked on the coals, and a cruse of water at his head. And so he did eat and drink, and lay down again. And the angel of the LORD came again the second time, and touched him, and said, Arise and eat; because the journey is too great for thee. And

he arose, and did eat and drink, and went in the strength of that meat forty days and forty nights unto Horeb, the mount of God."

First of all, notice that this treatment plan called for Elijah to be temporarily relieved of all his vocational responsibility. Today, such a goal is usually accomplished by hospitalizing the person. One of the primary benefits of hospitalizing the severely depressed person is to give him total rest.

Second, Elijah was put to sleep. Depressed people tend to extremes in their sleep patterns. Some may not be able to go to sleep. Once asleep, they may wake up frequently during the night, or they may awaken an hour or two before their normal rising time and be unable to go back to sleep. On the other hand, some depressed people want to sleep most of the time. Of course, neither of these extremes is healthy. However, adequate sleep is part of any successful treatment program.

Third, diet was a part of Elijah's treatment. A properly balanced diet is important in any recovery plan for depression.

Fourth, renewed spiritual vitality was at the heart of Elijah's treatment. Any Christian who has been depressed understands how important this element is to recovery.

I never will forget how my wife's battle with depression came to an end. We were holding evangelistic meetings in Beckley, West Virginia, and staying in the pastor's home. He and his wife had gone to make some hospital calls, so Dolores and I took advantage of our privacy to kneel for family devotions. That morning, while we were praying, she experienced a consciousness of God's presence. This was the first time in six months she had been free from the horribly haunting feeling of being totally forsaken by God.

There was nothing special about that morning to indicate what would happen. I certainly didn't expect anything like that to occur. I believed that she would get better. Although in my heart I knew she would be aware of God's presence again *some* day, I had no idea that it would happen that morning. But it did! That morning God touched her and lifted those heavy black clouds of depression from her.

This became obvious to me when she rose from her knees and came over to embrace me. There was energy in her face and a gleam in her eye. There was a lift in her voice as she said, "Honey, the Lord touched me this morning, and I feel so much better!" What a celebration we had! It would be several months before depression would be an uncommon part of her day, but its back was broken that morning.

There is often a significant biochemical involvement in deep depression such as my wife experienced. If you've ever gone through this with a family member, you know you reach a point where you can no longer communicate with that person. You try, but it's as though they can't hear what you say.

It will be easier for you to relate to your friends or loved ones compassionately if you understand that *they would communicate with you if they could, but they can't.* It's not so much that they are *unwilling* to communicate as it is that they are *unable.* Assuming that they are unwilling to communicate simply generates more frustration and anger on your part and makes it more difficult for you to be compassionate.

Be patient. In time, you will observe an obvious mood lift in them. Then, efforts to communicate will be much more likely to succeed.

Treating depression may require medication.

Today there are medications which can help alleviate depression and shorten its duration. Had these medications been available when my wife was suffering from depression, they could have brought her noticeable relief and considerably shortened that period of her life when she was so miserable.

Our center takes a conservative view toward the use of medication. However, under competent medical supervision, we have found it helpful in most cases where people are suffering from moderate to severe depression.

People who are taking medication for depression should be encouraged to take it as long as the doctor believes it is necessary, and at approximately the same time each day, so that at all times it can be as evenly distributed as possible in the body chemistry.

Often, depressed people neglect their medication. Some may even resist it because they see it as a symbol of their illness. The fewer pills they take, the more healthy they see themselves to be. The more medication they take and the longer they take it, the sicker they see themselves to be.

Of course, this is not an accurate perception of their situation. If they reduce their medication or quit taking it before they recover enough to function comfortably without it, their condition will very likely worsen. When medication is part of the treatment, it is important that it be prescribed by a competent physician, taken according to his instructions, and terminated only under his supervision.

Celebrate every bright spiritual moment.

For the Christian who is battling depression, it is important to celebrate any bright spiritual moment as evidence of God's help in the recovery process. However, care must be taken not to over-react. If a person attaches an exaggerated meaning to early moments of this nature and assumes they indicate an immediate end to the depression, any return of depression is likely to devastate his hope of recovery.

The pattern of recovery for most people involves a *gradual emergence* from depression. Little by little, the periods of relief grow longer and more frequent. The periods of depression are less frequent and less intense. Most often, this is the pattern we see as a person recovers from deep depression.

Long-range goals for depression-prone people.

Some Christians must have total success in every venture they undertake or they feel totally defeated. However, there is something to be said for even moderate improvement in those situations where total success may not be attainable.

If you are a depression-prone person and would like to be as free from depression as possible, let me suggest some long-range goals for you. Please understand that reaching these goals may not eliminate depression from your future, but it can minimize the toll depression takes on you.

1. See the advantages of depression.

For many people, depression is a primary way of coping with stress. As such, it is far less damaging than coping with stress through your cardiovascular or gastrointestinal system. When these systems become the primary channel for managing stress, you may end up with permanent damage to the vital organs involved.

As a means of coping with stress, therefore, depression does have some advantages. Once the misery of the mood has lifted, you are not as likely to have damaged your body as are those who manage stress through the major life-supporting systems of their body.

2. Learn to creatively manage your angry feelings.

Often, a large component of depression is anger trapped within a person and turned against oneself. A client we'll call Sue is a good example of how this can happen and how it affects a person's life over the years.

When Sue first came to see me, she had been experiencing depression throughout the Christmas holidays for several years. She couldn't understand why. Sue and her husband had a good marriage. Their children were healthy. The family was full of love and they enjoyed being together.

Sue's depression spoiled much of the joy of Christmas for the whole family, and she wanted to do something about it so that it wouldn't spoil another Christmas. We began to search for the source of her holiday depression . . . and it didn't take her long to discover it once she really got down to work.

Sue grew up in a large family. Her mother was an alcoholic. She remembered how, when she was a child, she dreamed of having a happy Christmas. But her mother was always drunk. There was no money for presents because it went for alcohol instead. There was no big family dinner. There were no cookies.

Their family holiday "tradition" was to get through the season without anybody finding out about her mother's alcoholism. Christmas was one of the most unhappy times of the year for her.

The special joy of the season that she read about in books and saw portrayed in Christmas programs never came to Sue's family. She could remember thinking, "I hate my mother. If she wanted to, she could make Christmas nice for us—but she would rather get drunk."

Sue had never dealt with this anger. She needed an opportunity to acknowledge it and get it out of her. She needed help forgiving herself for holding all that anger against her mother for so many years. Eventually, she had to come to the place where she could forgive her mother. When these issues were dealt with, Sue and her family had their first depression-free Christmas. What a changed individual we saw when she came to visit the Center after the next holiday season!

157

Once you are willing to acknowledge the fact that anger is playing a significant part in your depression, you have gone a long way toward doing something constructive about it. See if you can identify what it is you are angry about. Then, refer to Chapter 4 for some suggestions about how to manage your anger.

3. Work on adopting a positive world view.

Remember, the same glass of water which appears half empty to some appears half full to others. Why not join the group that sees it half full?

You can test the nature of your world view by noticing what aspects of the world's future you focus on. What phases of Bible prophecy most intrigue you? When your view of the future is positive, you assume that *"This world hasn't seen its best days yet—and neither have I!"*

Paul prescribes an effective "thought filter" for those who want to focus on the positive in life. In Philippians 4:8 (KJV) he writes:

"Finally, brethren, whatsoever things are true, whatsoever things are honest, whatsoever things are just, whatsoever things are pure, whatsoever things are lovely, whatsoever things are of good report; if there be any virtue, and if there be any praise, think on these things."

4. See the divine potential in other people.

Learn the thrill of seeing God in the lives of your family members. See Him in the circumstances of your friends' lives. Of course, the fortunes of this world and the power of Satan are working in our lives, too, but you still have a choice where you want to fix your focus.

Having a positive view of life has nothing to do with closing your eyes to the evil realities around you. You see them. You know they exist. But you do not choose to focus on them. You choose to focus on Christ because *"Greater is he that is in you than he that is in the world"* (1 John 4:4, KJV). The author of Hebrews says it so well: *"But now we see not yet all things put under him. But we see Jesus..."* (Hebrews 2:8,9, KJV).

Remember, Jesus is the door into life in another dimension. Don't be content merely to step *out of* an old life. Be determined to step *into* a new one. In the next chapter, I will share with you some of the exciting discoveries which await the Christian who is determined to explore his new dimension of life in Christ.

Chapter Seven

You Can Live in a New Dimension

. . . The Art of Creative Prayer

Many people allow their lives to be dominated by their physical and emotional desires. Generally, they do what they feel like doing. Others tend to feel *driven* by their life rather than being in control of it. Circumstances and other people determine their course. They do what they have to do to survive.

However, the Lord can help you turn your life around. He can help you put your spirit—under His control—in the driver's seat of your life. Life will be better for you when you learn to make Jesus the Lord of your choices and live a life of action rather than re-action, a life that acts on wise choices rather than simply reacting to what others and your circumstances dictate.

Donna discovered this secret in the face of impossible odds. When I first met her she was single, in her teens, and living in a wheelchair. The doctors gave her little hope of even surviving. She had suffered polio as a child and when we first met she was locked into what appeared to be a losing battle with tuberculosis.

161

"The doctors say I'm going to die," Donna volunteered as I arrived at her hospital bedside the first time. "It's not their fault, though. They're doing the best they can."

"What do you think about what the doctors have told you?" I asked.

"I think they're wrong," she said, with a twinkle in her eye.

That was over thirty years ago. Donna is still going strong. Her doctors *were* wrong. But that's not all they were wrong about. They discouraged her from getting married, and told her she could never give birth to a child.

In a day when *able-bodied* people often have difficulty finding a suitable mate, Donna has had *two*. Her first husband loved her very much and took care of her as long as he lived. He gave her two lovely children: one son and one daughter. Both are grown now. Their father is dead, and Donna has since married another man who thinks the sun rises and sets in her.

The last time I saw Donna, she was visiting a church where I was speaking. After the service we had a few moments to reminisce. "Donna," I said, "I have to tell you that the first time I saw you, I didn't think you were going to make it."

"I know," she snapped back with a chuckle. "You were just like the rest of the doctors. But I fooled you, didn't I?"

"You sure did," I admitted. "Now, if somebody told me you were *dead*, I wouldn't believe them."

"Well," she said humbly, "it's just the Lord. He's the one. He's brought me through."

That's the truth. God did provide the healing in her life. But Donna played a role in her own survival, too. The part she played is one that each of us can learn.

Donna learned how to keep her feelings from dominating her life. Now she has risen above the clumsiness and awkwardness of her crippled body. She refuses to be dominated by emotions which would give her little to feel good about. Much—if not most—of the time, her spirit has been in the driver's seat of her life.

Prayer is the door!

Prayer can open this new dimension of life to you. It's sad to think about how many believers *never discover this.* They approach prayer in a very traditional, ritualistic, and unimaginative way. For them, prayer remains a way of giving God His orders for the day. Some even have lists arranged just to be sure they don't miss anything. And when God doesn't do *what* they want Him to do, *when* they want Him to do it, they get *angry* with Him.

Such immature Christians seem to believe that God exists to do their will. Otherwise, why would they *blame God for the bad things that happen to them*—and the *good things which don't?*

Trust God for your material needs!

Make no mistake about it—God does encourage us to make our requests known to Him. But He also wants us to learn to trust Him more for our material needs so more of our prayer time can be devoted to seeking His kingdom.

Many of the things we pray for would come to us even if we didn't ask for them. Jesus teaches us that our material needs are met as by-products of putting Him first in our lives. In Matthew 6:31-33 (KJV), He states His priorities for our prayer times in a practical and powerful statement that can change our lives and help us change our world. He says:

"Therefore take no thought, saying, What shall we eat? or, What shall we drink? or, Wherewithal shall we be clothed? (For after all these things do the Gentiles seek:) for

your heavenly Father knoweth that ye have need of all these things. But seek ye first the kingdom of God and his righteousness; and all these things shall be added unto you."

What Jesus is talking about here can be called "creative prayer." It is recognizing the supremacy of the unseen over the seen, of spirit over matter. Science has taught us to respect the power of the unseen. The material secrets of the universe are hidden in the invisible forces of nature. For example, in my lifetime, the atom has been exploded and found to house an array of sub-atomic particles. Although this world of the atom cannot be seen by the naked eye, it contains the keys of life and death. In much the same way, the world of spirit holds the keys to the world of matter.

**Creative praying recognizes
the supremacy of spirit over matter.**

Spirit (God) preceded matter in existence. Spirit (God) is eternal and supreme over all, with no beginning and no end. Matter is temporal. It has a beginning and an ending. Therefore, all matter has come from spirit. Matter is to be subject to spirit.

Hebrews 11:3 (KJV) underscores these observations:

"Through faith we understand that the worlds were framed by the word of God, so that things which are seen were not made of things which do appear."

The Scriptures teach that beyond such invisible dynamics of the physical sciences there is an unseen spiritual power responsible for creating and sustaining the universe. John calls the Creator and Sustainer of the universe the "Logos." The power of the Logos is referred to as "zoe" in 1 John 1:4; Greek for "eternal life."

Eternal life is now!

Many Christians think of eternal life as a kind of existence which will begin for them when they die or when Jesus returns.

164

For example, the other day I heard a well-intentioned preacher refer to a believer's death as his "having entered into eternal life."

All of us look forward to being with the Lord. However, I want to help you discover that this dynamic gift of "eternal life" can enrich your life now.

Once you understand that eternal life is a creative power that is given to you by Jesus Christ, it will be easier for you to benefit from its function in your life while you are still in this world. God wants "eternal life" to be a prominent part of your Christian experience in the present.

Eternal life is the creative power from which God made the entire universe. John describes that manifestation of God's power in creation like this:

"In the beginning was the Word, and the Word was with God, and the Word was God. The same was in the beginning with God. All things were made by him; and without him was not anything made that was made. In him was life; and the life was the light of men" (John 1:1-4, KJV).

The Greek word for eternal life is "zoe," remember. The Greek word for natural, biological life is "bios." "Bios" occurs eleven times in the New Testament and each time it clearly refers to natural life. "Zoe" occurs 134 times in the New Testament. In all but eleven of these instances, it obviously refers to a supernatural kind of life. This is the power through which *"all things were made by him;"* the power through which Christ made all things from nothing. "Zoe" is spiritual and invisible in nature, so powerful that *the material universe is simply one of its manifestations.*

John tells us further that this creative force has always resided in Jesus. It was His manifestation of that life-creating

165

power in the beginning that resulted in all things being made out of nothing:

> *"And this is the testimony: God has given us eternal life, and this life is in his Son. He who has the Son has life; he who does not have the Son of God does not have life."*
>
> (1 John 5:11,12, NIV)

Jesus—as the eternal Word of God—is the source of this creative life or energy (zoe) from which everything that is made has come. With this understanding of who Jesus is and what eternal life is, read John 3:16,17 (KJV):

> *"For God so loved the world, that he gave his only begotten Son, that whosoever believeth in him should not perish, but have everlasting life. For God sent not his Son into the world to condemn the world; but that the world through him might be saved."*

What does this famous gospel text say to you? Its meaning is obvious, isn't it? As God's gift of love to this planet, Jesus came to give access to "eternal life" to all who believe in Him.

Why did God send that love gift?

In the beginning, God created man capable of mentally responding to this invisible creative force, "zoe." This is manifested in Adam's power of creative choice. Before the fall, he was able to name all the animals as they were brought before him:

> *"Now the LORD God had formed out of the ground all the beasts of the field and all the birds of the air. He brought them to the man to see what he would name them; and whatever the man called each living creature, that was its name. So the man gave names to all the livestock, the birds of the air and all the beasts of the field. But for Adam, no suitable helper was found"* (Genesis 2:19,20, NIV).

166

However, when Adam chose to eat of the tree of the knowledge of good and evil, he assumed the awesome responsibility of moral choice. Also, at that moment, he forfeited his access to eternal life. That part of Adam's spirit capable of responding to eternal life became dead in *"trespasses and sins."*

"As for you, you were dead in your transgressions and sins, in which you used to live when you followed the ways of this world and of the ruler of the kingdom of the air, the spirit who is now at work in those who are disobedient."

(Ephesians 2:1, NIV)

This is the death God warned Adam of in Genesis 2:15-17 (KJV):

"And the LORD God took the man, and put him into the Garden of Eden to dress it and to keep it. And the LORD God commanded the man, saying, Of every tree of the garden thou mayest freely eat; But of the tree of the knowledge of good and evil, thou shalt not eat of it: for in the day that thou eatest thereof, thou shalt surely die."

This state of spiritual death has been transmitted from Adam to his offspring so that *"in Adam all die"* (1 Corinthians 15:22). However, God's love for mankind is so great that He offered His Son Jesus to die for the sins of Adam and his race. By accepting Christ's death and resurrection as an atonement for their sins, anyone who wants to can be born again (John 3:17).

What part of you becomes born again?

The part of you that is born again is that part of your spirit and mind which has been dead as a result of sin. Once you are born again, you are capable of responding to eternal life. Your regenerated sensitivity to eternal life enables you to experience the love of the Father, the triumphant presence of the Son, and the teaching ministry of the Holy Spirit.

Remember, eternal life is an invisible power which resides in Jesus Christ. When you are born again, your spirit becomes sensitive to this life and it stimulates your mind. You begin to think in terms of life options that enhance and develop your divine potential.

Your spirit is also sensitive to sin as it impacts on your mind. Sin stimulates your brain to think in terms of life options that detract from and destroy your divine potential.

Many Christians I see in counseling have trouble relating these spiritual forces to the daily issues of their lives. They do not understand that there is a spiritual dimension to their thoughts. Thinking is such a common experience to them, they assume it to be totally natural.

However, temptation and divine suggestion—both supernatural in origin—present themselves to each of us through our thoughts, imaginations, and urges. *Temptation* is the product of an invisible power emanating from *Satan* which we call *sin*. *Divine suggestion* results from the invisible power emanating from *Jesus Christ* which we call *eternal life*.

Unfortunately, the average church member is more aware of temptation than he is of divine suggestion. Since he is so unaware of divine suggestion, he often feels overwhelmed by the complexities and ambiguities of today's world.

As a result, he often suffers from uncomfortable levels of anxiety. A practical understanding of the power of eternal life and how it enters into his daily decisions can eliminate much of this anxiety.

For centuries, Christians have believed that human history is shaped by two spiritual forces: satanic and divine. Although most agree that both powers are governed by God's providential love, Christians differ over how much personal freedom exists and where human responsibility lies within their jurisdiction.

However, there is general agreement that man is sufficiently free to be held accountable before God. Most theologians believe our behavior results from our interaction with these spiritual powers in our mind.

The Bible illustrates how human decisions often were involved in the execution of providence. Reflecting on this aspect of history, Golda Meir, former prime minister of Israel, is said to have jokingly complained, "Just think, if Moses had turned left rather than right after he crossed the Red Sea, we would have had all the oil and they [the Arabs] would have had all the rocks!"

As God providentially rules the course of all human history through His access to man's decision-making process, so He wants to guide each of us in the critical decisions of our daily lives.

"For as many as are led by the Spirit of God, they are the sons of God" (Romans 8:14, KJV).

Through creative prayer, the believer becomes aware of spiritual activity in his thought processes. He develops the ability to know the difference between those thoughts resulting from sin, those originating from eternal life, and those suggested by his own natural thought processes.

Scripture stored in memory is an invaluable tool for discerning the spiritual origin of our thoughts. And whether you consider Hebrews 4:12 (KJV) to refer primarily to the *written* Word of God or the *living* Word of God, its truth remains:

"For the word of God is quick, and powerful, and sharper than any two-edged sword, piercing even to the dividing asunder of soul and spirit, and of the joints and marrow, and is a discerner of the thoughts and intents of the heart."

169

Skill in discerning the spiritual origin of your thoughts develops as the living Word is enthroned in your spirit and the written Word is stored in your memory.

Why should a person engage in creative praying?

The idea of eternal life as an invisible power capable of stimulating creative thoughts and choices for life may sound mystical to some. However, belief in invisible forces *in nature* is a commonly accepted part of life.

Wind, a vacuum, and electricity are just a few examples of invisible natural forces which have a profound impact on us. This is possible because we have discovered enough about their principles and properties to develop the technology that enables us to benefit from their power.

Creative praying is based on the assumption that *invisible spiritual powers* are at least as active as *invisible natural forces* in shaping the events of our world—and just as predictable in the ways they operate. The Bible defines the principles and properties of "sin" and "eternal life," invisible spiritual powers. By tapping into this Biblical truth, the believer can gain an understanding of these powers that enables him to understand their relationships to the practical issues of life.

Through prayer and your study of Scripture, you can become more aware of these spiritual powers. You can learn how they affect your thought processes and the choices which shape your life and destiny. Let's look at some of the ways creative prayer will make a difference in your life.

1.   Creative prayer helps to make you a new creation.

Through creative praying, children of Adam become children of God (John 1:12). We never pray a more creative prayer than when we ask God to forgive our sins and enable us to be born again. Acknowledging our personal need of the atonement

170

of Christ's death and resurrection not only makes it possible for our sins to be forgiven; it also enables us to become *dead to sin* and *alive to eternal life.*

In Christ, we are becoming ever more dead and insensitive to the destructive options for living that "sin" stimulates in our minds. And we are becoming more and more sensitive to the creative options for living suggested to our minds by "eternal life."

This is what "putting off the old man" and "putting on the new man" is all about. Paul refers to this process as being *"renewed in the spirit of your mind"* (Ephesians 4:23, KJV). There is no greater miracle than this!

Can you remember what it was like before you knew Christ as Savior? Can you remember the contrast between your life then and now? What could you possibly ask of God which would require a greater miracle? Here is how Paul describes the difference this miracle makes in us:

"And you hath he quickened, who were dead in trespasses and sins; Wherein in time past ye walked according to the course of this world, according to the prince of the power of the air, the spirit that now worketh in the children of disobedience: Among whom also we all had our conversation in times past in the lusts of our flesh, fulfilling the desires of the flesh and of the mind; and were by nature the children of wrath, even as others.

"But God, who is rich in mercy, for his great love wherewith he loved us, Even when we were dead in sins, hath quickened us together with Christ, (by grace ye are saved;) and hath raised us up together and made us sit together in heavenly places in Christ Jesus: That in the ages to come he might shew the exceeding riches of his grace in his kindness toward us through Christ Jesus. For by grace

*are ye saved through faith; and that not of yourselves: it is
the gift of God: Not of works, lest any man should boast."*
(Ephesians 2:1-9, KJV)

2. **Creative prayer changes the way you view your
past.**

When you are born again, the hurts of your past are not
always automatically and instantly healed. *Being born again is
the initial treatment of an ailing life; it is not the total cure.*

Many begin their Christian life with unpleasant memories
from the past. Often these have left painfully deep marks on us.
Such old hurts need to be healed so that we do not
unconsciously—or, perhaps, consciously—cling to them with all
their pain. Unless we surrender old hurts to Christ, they can get
in the way of the future God has planned for us.

While the *facts* of your personal history do remain fixed,
you can change the way you choose to *feel* and *think* about
those facts. You can change the way you are affected by what
has happened to you in the past. *You don't have to be a prisoner
of your past.*

Every year, I talk to hundreds of believers who have brought
with them into God's kingdom bitterness, disappointment, anger,
fear, envy, jealousy, or other damaging feelings. Such pain may
have its roots in things which have happened in their family, a
former marriage, a job situation, or a church squabble. They may
feel that their parents abused or mistreated them, their brothers
and sisters were unfair to them, their former mate took advantage
of them, a business partner cheated them, or people in the church
gossiped about them. These are the kinds of things that fester in
people's spirits and poison their lives.

What are your pains from yesterday which tend to spill
over into your today and threaten your tomorrows? How are you
interpreting them? God can help you discover new and creative

172

ways of viewing them through the options He stimulates in your mind by eternal life.

By choosing to see your old hurts His way, you will become a *better* person rather than a *bitter* person. Notice, the difference between bitter and better is just one letter, "I." "I" make the difference between my becoming a bitter person or a better person by the way "I" choose to react to and think about the things not of my own choosing which have happened to me in life.

3. **Creative prayer changes the way you view your external world.**

It is amazing how different our external world looks once our internal world of remembrances and thoughts is comfortable. Many problems with others simply disappear. You see, problems *between people* usually have their roots in problems *within people.*

Back in the days when everybody hung their washing out on the clothes line, a dear lady used to complain about her neighbor's dirty wash—until the day she cleaned her own windows. The internal perspective from which you view your world affects both what you see and how you see it.

As in Israel's day (Numbers 13:33), when some people peer into the Promised Land of their tomorrows, they see it full of giants so tall as to make them feel like grasshoppers. Others look at the same situation, discover a land that flows with *"milk and honey"* (Numbers 13:27,30), and are confident they can conquer it.

When your thoughts about your present situation are stimulated by eternal life, you will know it. You will be thinking of your circumstances in the most positive way. A healthy person doesn't attempt to deal with the harsh realities of life by continually denying them. Rather, with God's help, he learns to view them as positively as possible. These creative vantage points are often revealed to the believer during times of prayer and meditation.

4. Creative prayer helps you to change the external realities of your life.

God seldom performs miracles that *affect* men without *involving* men in the working of those miracles. Many people do not want to assume any responsibility for the circumstances in their lives. And they feel so overwhelmed . . . they don't see how they can assume *any* responsibility for changing their circumstance.

They blame their unhappiness on others—their parents, their brothers and sisters, their friends, their mates or former mates, their children, or the devil. The list is endless. In their eyes, they are not responsible for what has happened to them and they are not able to do anything about it. Only God can deliver them!

This kind of passive-dependent person is a bystander in his own life! Someone has said there are basically three kinds of people in the world: people who make things happen, people who watch things happen, and people who never quite figure out what is happening.

Passive-dependent people never seem to get out of the grandstand of life. Usually they are fearful and angry, afraid of the responsibilities of life and angry at others for not doing more to help them.

These people often see their problems as the work of the devil; therefore, they insist that only the Lord can *solve* their problems. Satan causes them and Jesus takes them away, while the person himself remains passive during the whole magical process. Unfortunately, the naive and indiscriminate believer

174

frequently sees people who talk like this as being deeply spiritual. In most cases, nothing could be farther from the truth.

Eternal life is not magic!

Eternal life is an *invisible supernatural power,* but it is *neither magical nor superstitious.* It is a dimension of reality in which God does His work in His world at levels of understanding beyond our comprehension.

Isaiah expressed it this way:

> *"For my thoughts are not your thoughts, neither are your ways my ways, saith the LORD. For as the heavens are higher than the earth, so are my ways higher than your ways, and my thoughts than your thoughts."*
>
> (Isaiah 55:8,9, KJV)

Once we become aware of the impact of eternal life on our thought processes, God wants us to be involved with Him in the miracles that affect our lives. Paul says it this way:

> *"Work out your own salvation with fear and trembling. For it is God which worketh in you both to will and to do of his good pleasure"* (Philippians 2:12,13, KJV).

The fact that we are involved makes what happens no less supernatural. Paul assures us of this:

> *"Now unto him that is able to do exceeding abundantly above all that we ask or think, according to the power that worketh in us"* (Ephesians 3:20, KJV).

God never asks us to do what He knows we can't. But as we put the *possible* in His hand, He uses it to do the *impossible.* When Moses stretched out his rod toward the Red Sea, God parted the water. When Israel was willing to march around the walls of Jericho, God tore the walls down. When the servants at the marriage at Cana were willing to fill the waterpots with water,

175

Jesus turned the water into wine. When one lad gave the Lord his five loaves and two fish, Jesus used it to feed five thousand men plus the women and children who were with them in the desert (Matthew 14:14-21).

People who just want to pray and let God do it all are exposing themselves to the risk of devastating disappointments.

Prayer—by itself—seldom changes things.

Prayer usually changes *people*—and *people change things*. Don't misunderstand. God can do all things. However, He has chosen us to become *"workers together with him"* (2 Corinthians 6:1, KJV). This is why God seldom performs a miracle which *affects* men without *involving* them.

By engaging in creative prayer, ordinary people like you and I can learn how to become involved with God in extraordinary manifestations of eternal life in our world.

How does a person pray creatively?

First, commit God's Word to memory. How much Scripture do you know by memory? How long has it been since you have stored a new verse of God's Word in your mind? Remember, God's Word is creative. If you want your prayers to be creative, you will want to involve both the living and written Word of God in them.

David found that hiding God's Word in his heart helped him build up an internal resistance to the destructive attitudes and habits that sin tried to generate in his life. He wrote in Psalm 119:11 (KJV), *"Thy word have I hid in mine heart, that I might not sin against thee."*

In addition to building up resistance to sin's destructive habits and attitudes, Scripture committed to memory serves a second very important purpose in the believer's life. It becomes a creative resource which can surface at just the right moment to help you define otherwise undiscovered options for living (John 14:26).

Second, spend time listening in prayer. For some people, prayer is an exercise in one-way communication where God does all the listening and all the obeying. When they are finished talking to God, they are finished praying.

Yet very often, in Scripture, the believer is instructed to wait on God and listen to God speak to him in return. In Revelation 2:7 (KJV) Jesus admonishes, *"He that hath an ear to hear, let him hear what the Spirit saith unto the churches...."*

In Luke 8:18 (KJV), He advises His disciples, *"Take heed... how ye hear."*

Learning to listen in prayer.

At first when you start to listen in prayer, you may find it difficult to hear. So, let me suggest you begin by determining that you will spend half of your prayer time in listening. Just make that a standard practice of your prayer life. For example, if you are in the habit of spending ten minutes a day in prayer, then spend the first five minutes talking to God and the last five minutes letting Him talk to you.

When you begin to develop the art of listening in prayer, don't be surprised to discover a thousand voices filling the silence. The worries of yesterday, the cares of today, the fears of tomorrow, all will try to come crashing in on you. Just as Paul explained in 1 Thessalonians 4:11, you will have to *"study to be quiet."*

Practice is essential if you are to develop this spiritual skill. However, in time, the Lord will help you to become proficient in:

"Casting down imaginations, and every high thing that exalteth itself against the knowledge of God, and bringing into captivity every thought to the obedience of Christ."
(2 Corinthians 10:5)

177

Only as we learn to hear what God is saying to us in prayer do we begin to tap into the creative dimension of prayer. The psalmist certainly understood this. He shares with us what the Lord taught him: *"Be still, and know that I am God"* (Psalm 46:10, KJV).

Americans are conditioned to a noisy life. When most of us wake up in the morning, we turn on the radio or television to provide our morning noise. In fact, some of us are wakened by the radio. Many of us cannot stand the stillness in our automobiles. No sooner do we get in the car and crank up the engine than we turn on the radio. The last thing turned off at night in many homes is the radio or television. From the time we get out of bed in the morning until we crawl back into bed at night, many of us demonstrate that we are more comfortable with noise than with silence.

Even in our churches, there is very little silence. The organ is playing. Someone is singing. Someone is making announcements. The preacher is speaking. Many of us are so unaccustomed to silence in worship that we would find it extremely awkward.

God wants us to seek out some quiet time. He urges us to develop the ability to quiet ourselves and listen to what the Holy Spirit would say to us.

Mental fatigue is common among the people I see. They are bombarded with stimuli from waking to sleeping. Consequently, their ability to distinguish trivia from vital relationship issues is impaired. Millions of sights and sounds compete for their attention every day. People are tired even when their bodies are rested.

Few have learned how to *rest the mind.* One way of doing this is to develop the art of prayerful "listening." Nothing is more restful and refreshing than quiet time before God. Isaiah discovered:

"They that wait upon the LORD shall renew their strength; they shall mount up with wings as eagles; they shall run, and not be weary; and they shall walk and not faint" (Isaiah 40:31).

"Wait upon the Lord."

Meditation is one of the oldest forms of Christian worship and prayer. While Western Christianity has neglected this ancient tradition of the church, other religions are using it effectively as a means of attracting mentally tired Americans through the serenity which meditation offers.

Today, meditation is so often associated with Eastern religions that some believers are reluctant to practice it. They fear that others might think they are contaminating their Christian faith with some New Age practice. However, Scripture is clear that God wants His people to enjoy the benefits of meditation. David describes the "blessed" or happy man as one whose *"... delight is in the law of the LORD; and in his law doth he meditate day and night"* (Psalm 1:2, KJV).

Some of the most creative moments of my life have come after I have talked to God, praised Him, thanked Him, worshipped Him, and then sat quietly to listen to what He would say to me through His Spirit and from His Word. Once you have developed the ability to wait and listen, you won't want to pray without some time for meditation. For years, I have spent *more time listening than talking* in prayer.

Learn to listen.

If you are a beginner in learning to pray creatively, let me suggest that you take the first two or three minutes of your prayer time for quiet praise. Then, spend the next three or four minutes talking to God about your concerns. After that, rest your mind by committing all your cares to Jesus. Develop skill in following Peter's advice, *"Casting all your care upon him; for he careth for you"* (1 Peter 5:7, KJV).

Focus your thoughts on a peaceful Bible scene or a restful verse of Scripture and wait quietly before the Lord. Learn to take advantage of those unplanned moments that come to you through the day by using them as opportunities for meditation.

For example, most of us can get along very well with four and one-half hours of deep sleep. Sometimes I wake up at 5:30 or 6:00 in the morning. I already have the hours of sleep I require. What am I going to do? I have several options. I can begin to wonder why I can't go back to sleep. I can become very upset and frustrated because someone or something has disturbed me early in the morning and robbed me of my sleep. Or, I can take advantage of this unexpected quiet time in the presence of the Lord and listen for what He may say to me.

Often in such moments the Lord will remind me of people to pray for. Sometimes He brings to my attention a situation that I need to take care of and help me see it in a way I had not considered. Frequently, with such a new perspective, the Lord also will suggest options for problem-solving that I had not thought of before. The wisdom He suggests to us in creative moments like these makes our smartest thoughts appear foolish.

It is at such times the Lord may show you new ways of feeling and thinking about some old hurts in your own life, and help you to change your views about people and events in your past which have caused you pain.

Creative prayer can heal wounded relationships!

It was during such a sleepless night that God healed Jacob of the ill feelings he had toward Esau (Genesis 32). Jacob was a great one for believing that his troubles were caused by others. So, as he was coming back from his uncle Laban's, he remembered that he would soon have to meet his brother Esau. It had been years since the two had seen each other.

The last time they were together, Esau had threatened to kill Jacob. Do you remember how Jacob had collaborated with their mother, Rebecca, to swindle Esau's blessing from their father, Isaac? Esau had been enraged ... and Jacob believed Esau had kept that grudge alive for fourteen years.

Jacob concocted an elaborate scheme to make peace with his brother. He sent offerings of animals to Esau. Then he strategically arranged his servants, his wives, and even his children in a spectacular parade of appeasement. Each group had a carefully prepared speech, designed to convince Esau that Jacob considered himself to be Esau's servant.

Jacob was still so afraid, even after he had organized this gigantic parade, that he sneaked off to spend the night on the other side of the brook. God sent an angel to confront him there, and Jacob wrestled with the angel all night. As the dawn of Jacob's dreaded day began to break, the angel protested, *"Let me go"* (Genesis 32:26, KJV).

Afraid for his life, Jacob gripped the angel and cried, *"I will not let thee go except thou bless me"* (Genesis 32:26, KJV).

The angel responded by asking, *"What is thy name?"* (Genesis 32:27, KJV). Jacob was being asked to honestly reflect on what characterized him, what defined his personality, and what behavior those who knew him had come to expect from him. This question forced Jacob to face the real source of his problems for the first time in his life. He could no longer blame them on his father, his mother, his brother, or his uncle. He had to confront the fact that he was what his name implied—a deceiver and supplanter. After that night, Jacob would never be the same again. Finally, he faced the real source of his troubles: himself.

Notice what happened the morning after Jacob had that all-night wrestling match with the angel. When he faced Esau, who was it that made the first move toward whom? Who kissed whom first? It was Esau who threw his arms around Jacob. It was Esau who kissed Jacob.

Jacob discovered that Esau had forgiven him years before. Esau had put those painful experiences behind him. It was Jacob who had harbored the grudge and kept it alive in his mind. Just think of the needless torture he had heaped upon himself through the years!

Ever since the fall of Adam, we have all tended to identify our own problems—in other people! Children blame their problems on their parents. When divorce tears up a marriage, both partners tend to believe their divorce was mostly due to their mate's shortcomings or misbehavior. When people are fired, they explain it to themselves by accusing the supervisor of being unfair.

Of course, there are rare instances in life where each of these explanations might be accurate. However, it is a creative miracle when God helps us to see that the problems we have with others may largely be our own problems, and the changes which need to take place are mostly ours to make.

If a person is ever to be happy (remember, that is what being "blessed" means), he must have the courage to face his problems as they really are. There comes a time when God confronts each of us with the same question the angel posed for Jacob: *"What is your name?"*

In that moment, we need to face ourselves with the level of honesty portrayed in the old "spiritual" song: *"Not the preacher, nor the deacon, but it's me, O Lord, standin' in the need of prayer."*

182

Creative prayer helps in problem solving.

Creative prayer can help you discover new alternatives for solving the problems confronting you. It can also help you define new options for decisions you have to make.

In moments of meditation, learn to focus your thoughts on the matters demanding some judgment or decision from you. In each case, begin to define the options your own wisdom and experience suggest. In your imagination, project each of these options far enough into the future to anticipate its ultimate conclusion. If you are tuned in to your own thoughts during such a process, you can hear yourself thinking, "If I were to do this, then that would happen. And then that would follow. And then that would take place."

Pursue this same procedure with each option until you can—as nearly as possible—assess the consequences each of them might produce. Often, the Holy Spirit either will give you a fascination for an option you have defined through this process, or, through the creative power of eternal life, He will stimulate an option to your mind which had not previously occurred to you.

How will you know the difference between foolish thoughts which may surface in your mind during these moments of meditation and creative ways of viewing your situation which eternal life may stimulate? That distinction can be made more simply than you may imagine.

First of all, *suggestions stimulated by eternal life are always consistent with Scripture.*

Second, *options stimulated by eternal life will improve your relationships with the significant people in your life.* God will never lead you to do anything that would destroy a Christian marriage or family. He will never lead you to do anything that would embarrass the Body of Christ. He will never prompt you to be harmful to your neighbors or yourself. Any suggestions eternal life may introduce will be consistent with the most redemptive possible way of approaching the circumstances and relationships of your life.

Third, *divine suggestions will lend themselves to making you more effective in doing what God has called you to do.* God is glorified when you excel in the expression of the gifts and talents He has given you.

Fourth, *what eternal life suggests is practical.* It works! Often, when wisdom finally surfaces, it is so obviously appropriate that we wonder why we didn't think of it sooner. However, never let the practicality of a creative suggestion diminish your appreciation of its supernatural origin.

Some people can only see God in the spectacular. At times He does move in spectacular ways; more often, however, He moves through the regular channels of the routine matters of our lives.

As you develop an appreciation for God's guidance in the practical issues of your life, you will be excited to discover how frequently you find Him there.

You *can* sort it all out.

It will take practice for you to develop skill in sorting out divine suggestions from your own thoughts. In the process, you may do a foolish thing or two. Be patient with yourself. That is a small price to pay for the thrill of experiencing divine guidance in your life.

The author of Hebrews reminds us that few believers are willing to take this risk; but those who do are promised improved skill in discernment with practice.

"For when for the time ye ought to be teachers, ye have need that one teach you again which be the first principles of the oracles of God; and are become such as have need of milk, and not of strong meat. For every one that useth milk is unskillful in the word of righteousness: for he is a babe. But strong meat belongeth to them that are of full age, even those who by reason of use have their senses exercised to discern both good and evil" (Hebrews 5:12-14, KJV).

Here you are assured that as you practice the art of discerning good and evil in your thoughts, the Holy Spirit will help you become increasingly skilled in knowing which of your thoughts are the result of the confusion in and around you, which are the product of sin, which are the result of too much pizza before bedtime, and which are the creative voice of eternal life guiding you in God's best path.

Tomorrow's resources are unlimited!

The resources with which you face your tomorrows are not limited to the options of your own mind. Remember that you have access to the mind of Christ—which makes the wisdom of man look like foolishness (1 Corinthians 2:16, KJV):

"For who has known the mind of the LORD, that he may instruct him? But we have the mind of Christ."

The unlimited power of eternal life that makes man's greatest strength look like weakness (1 Corinthians 1:25) is at your disposal. Learning how to draw from these resources in making major life decisions is a practical explanation of what walking in the Spirit is all about.

Remember when God called Peter to invite Gentiles into the kingdom? Peter felt he could never do that. As a Jew, he naturally wanted the church to stay Jewish. If he had not been willing to put aside his personal bias, he would have missed that wonderful opportunity.

185

The Biblical account of this story is in the Book of Acts, chapter ten. There we are told that one day, while Peter was keeping his time of prayer, he drifted off to sleep. In that trance-like state between waking and sleeping, the Lord gave Peter one of the most creative moments of his life.

In a vision, Peter saw a large sheet let down from heaven. On it were all kinds of animals and birds. A voice said to Peter, *"Kill, and eat"* (Acts 10:13, NIV).

Peter responded with revulsion (v. 14): *" 'Surely not, Lord!' Peter replied. 'I have never eaten anything impure or unclean.' "*

Then, in that creative moment, the Lord said to Peter, *"What I have cleansed is not for you to call common or unclean (v. 15)."* A whole new dimension of ministry opened to Peter that day. He was awakened by a call from those who had come to take him to Cornelius' house so the Gentiles could hear the gospel.

Down to the house of Cornelius Peter went. He couldn't even finish his gospel message to them before the Spirit of God fell on this group of Gentiles. Back to the brethren at Jerusalem Peter came with the news that what had happened in Jerusalem on the Day of Pentecost had happened to the Gentiles.

It would have happened even if Peter had not gone, but Peter would have missed his chance to be a part of it. Because he was willing to involve himself in carrying out such a creative suggestion, he had the thrill of seeing the gospel introduced to the Gentiles.

A new dimension of living can open to you!

I challenge you to become aware of the activity of eternal life in your thought processes. Look at prayer differently than you have before. Begin to spend at least as much time listening to God as you spend talking to Him. If your todays are still suffering from yesterday's hurts, then in quiet, creative moments of prayer, let the Lord show you some healing ways to view your past. Nothing that has happened in your past needs to get in the way of God's best for your future.

Learn to identify the voice of the Lord in your thoughts. Involve His options in the problem-solving situations of your life. The decision-making opportunities of your tomorrows can be more exciting and challenging for you as you learn how to become involved with the Lord in the process of discovering His will.

In those creative moments you have with Him, sharpen your skills in hearing what He is saying to you. And, *"Whatsoever he saith unto you, do it"* (John 2:5, KJV). As you do, you will discover yourself to be celebrating life in a new dimension!

187

Chapter One
How Healthy Is Your Faith?

1. In what ways is life more complex today than when
    our grandparents and parents were children? Identify
    some of the unhealthy changes in our society.

2. Identify and discuss ways in which a person's faith
    and emotional health affect each other.

3. How does a healthy faith help a person deal with
    mental health problems and live a more integrated
    life?

4. Review and discuss the ten ways of testing your faith
    as given by Dr. Dobbins.

5. Each of us lives with the "story" we tell ourselves
    about the painful events of our lives. In what ways can
    a healthy faith help you look at these events
    differently?

6. Fear of change can hinder personal growth. In what
    ways can healthy faith accommodate change without
    compromising our relationship with Jesus?

7. Does mature love flow from weakness or strength?
    Explain.

Chapter Two
You Can Change Your Self-Concept

1. Read 1 Corinthians 6:19,20 and 1 Peter 1:18,19.
    According to these verses, what ultimately
    establishes our worth? How does this recognition
    foster healthy self-worth in our lives?

2. Where do our feelings about ourselves come from?

3. How do parents affect a child's self-image? What role
    do we play in the formation of our own self-images?

4. Read 1 Corinthians 13:12. Dr. Dobbins referred to our
    self-image as a "lens" through which we view
    ourselves and the events of life. How does our "lens"
    (our self-image) become distorted?

5. Read Proverbs 23:7 (KJV). What does this verse show
    us of the power of the self-image? In what ways will a
    healthy self-image be shown in a person's behaviors?
    In what ways will an unhealthy self-image be shown?

6. Persons suffering from a destructive self-image
    often believe their happiness is in the control of
    someone else. Why is this a deception, and how might
    it be harmful?

7. The first step in changing your self-image is to see
    yourself as a person God loves very much. Read
    Romans 5:6-9, John 3:16, and Galatians 2:19,20).
    Discuss what these verses say of God's love for you.

8. A second step in changing the self-image involves seeing ourselves as valuable to God. What is the difference between being "unprofitable" and being "worthless"? How will differentiating between the two help a person who suffers from low self-worth?

9. The third step to changing an unhealthy self-image is to come to the realization that God sees us as forgivable people. Sometimes it is easier to *believe* God has forgiven us than it is to *feel* that He has. Why is that?

10. Seeing ourselves as people capable of making necessary changes with God's help is the fourth step in changing our self-image. How does surrendering our pain to God begin the process of changing the "lens" through which we view life? Why would we prefer God to do all the work of changing our self-image?

Chapter Three
"Nothing to Fear but Fear Itself"

1. In what ways can fear and anxiety be healthy?

2. When do our fears and anxieties become *unhealthy?*

3. Where do our fears come from?

4. What is meant by the term "boundaries"? Why is it important to set physical, social, and spiritual boundaries for our lives? Read Proverbs 29:18 again and discuss its connection with the concept of "boundaries."

5. In what ways can fear and anxiety be detrimental to us physically and emotionally?

6. What are some of the natural controls for anxiety that God has given us? What is the "statistical perspective" method of controlling fear?

7. How can mentally focusing on reassuring passages of Scripture help alleviate fear and anxiety? Give examples of especially helpful passages you focus on in times of stress.

8. Read 2 Timothy 1:7 and discuss its connection with self-consciousness.

Chapter Four
Anger: Master or Servant?

1. In Mark 3:1–6, there are two very different expressions of anger shown. In what ways were the expressions of anger different as practiced by Jesus and the Pharisees?

2. Accepting anger as a fact of life is the first step toward living more comfortably with our anger. What guideline does Ephesians 4:26 give us regarding our anger? What type of angry expression should we feel guilty for?

3. How is unrecognized anger dangerous? Where are some of the places anger hides, according to Chapter Four of this text?

4. Dr. Dobbins suggested that anger is often hidden beneath words such as *I'm fed up* or *I'm hurt*. What are reasons that Christians might have for disguising anger with such words and phrases?

5. What are the two extremes we tend to go to when attempting to control our anger? What are the dangers of each of these extremes?

6. What are some of the benefits a person will enjoy from practicing some of the anger-control exercises mentioned in the text? (For example: going for a walk, quoting the Lord's Prayer, counting to ten.) In what ways are our lives complicated when we "shoot from the lip"?

7. What are some suggestions for sublimating anger's energy into worthwhile causes? Why is it important to channel anger's energy in a positive direction?

8. Why is it important to celebrate progress made in overcoming angry outbursts? What are some tangible ways of charting growth in this area?

Chapter Five
Coming to Terms With Guilt

1. What are the three characteristics of a healthy conscience given by Dr. Dobbins?

2. Where does the conscience come from? How and when is it developed within a person?

3. What effects do extremes in physical boundaries (too broad or too rigid) have on the conscience formation of small children?

4. What are the differences between punishment and discipline? Is it possible to have one without the other? What role does affirmation play in discipline?

5. Review and discuss the three-step formula (Three "F's" of good discipline) given for setting limits that will most likely result in the formation of a healthy conscience.

6. The conscience, like the self-image, is stable over time and highly resistant to change. How can this stability and resistance to change be both positive and negative?

7. What is the A-B-C method of treating an unhealthy conscience?

8. List and discuss the three characteristics differentiating healthy guilt from unhealthy guilt.

Chapter Six
Dealing with Depression

1. What are some reasons why the day in which we live might be referred to as "the age of depression"?

2. What is depression and what are some of its characteristics?

3. What effect does a person's self-image have upon depression?

4. Who suffers from depression? Identify and discuss Bible characters who suffered from depression.

5. Personal loss can precipitate a grief reaction. What are the four predictable stages a person will pass through, as identified by Dr. Dobbins? How long does it normally take to work through the stages involved with a grief reaction? How is it helpful to those experiencing a grief reaction to know that it may take a number of months to feel like themselves again?

6. Some forms of depression require medication as a part of their management. What might make it difficult for some to view medication for depression on the same plane as medications for other physical ailments (such as insulin for diabetes)?

7. How does our view of life affect our proneness toward depression?

8. What are the suggestions for dealing with depression as given in the text? What role does talking to others play in overcoming depression? What value does recreation (learning to play) have in helping offset depression?

Chapter Seven
You Can Live in a New Dimension

1. How does prayer serve as a door to living in a new dimension? What changes are made in a person's life through the use of creative prayer?

2. What is "eternal life" (zoe) and in what ways does it affect our lives here on earth? What impact does it have upon our daily thoughts and decisions?

3. Why is it important for us as Christians to develop the ability to know the difference between those thoughts resulting from sin, those originating from eternal life, and those suggested by our own natural thought processes?

4. What are the steps involved with creative prayer? How does creative prayer help heal broken relationships and painful memories?

5. What are the guidelines by which we can distinguish between our own "foolish thoughts" and "creative options" stimulated by eternal life during our moments of meditation?

6. Living in a new dimension requires commitment and effort. As you have been reading this chapter, what areas of your life has the Spirit of God prompted you to give attention to?